MOONCAKES AND HUNGRY GHOSTS

FESTIVALS OF CHINA

Carol Stepanchuk
and Charles Wong

CHINA BOOKS & PERIODICALS • SAN FRANCISCO

We are grateful to the following publishers for permission to use extended quotations from these works: *China Men*, by Maxine Hong Kingston. Copyright © 1977, 1978, 1979, 1980 by Maxine Hong Kingston. Reprinted by permission of Alfred A. Knopf, Inc. *The Joy Luck Club*, by Amy Tan. Reprinted by permission of the Putnam Publishing Group. Copyright © 1989 by Amy Tan. *Monkey*, by Authur Waley. Grove Press, 1980. *Unities and Diversities in Chinese Religion*, by Robert P. Weller. University of Washington Press, 1987. *A Traveler in China*, by Christina Dodwell. Beaufort Books, 1987.

Photo credits: pp. 4 — Asian Art Museum. Color plates 2a, 2b, 3a, 9a; pp. 6, 7, 11, 14, 15, 16, 18, 23, 37, 40, 60 — Po Sung-nien. Color plates 1a, 1b; p. 27 — Kim Raftery. Color plates 10b, 11; pp. 112, 113 — China Tourism. Color plates 3b, 4a, 4b; pp. 63, 64, 72, 73, 74, 88, 129, 130 – Al Cohen. pp. 63, 111, 131 — Al Dien. Color plate 7 — Charlotte Temple. Color plates 10a, 12a, 12b — How Man Wong.

Cover design by Wendy K. Lee
Text design by Linda Revel
Additional illustrations by Wendy K. Lee

Copyright © 1991 by Carol Stepanchuk and Charles Wong

First edition 1991

3 5 7 9 10 8 6 4

Library of Congress Catalog Card Number: 91-73127
ISBN 0-8351-2481-9

Printed in Hong Kong by Regent Publishing Services, Ltd.
Published in the United States of America by CHINA BOOKS & Periodicals, Inc.

To Bob and Sarah,
with whom I celebrate . . .
— *C. S.*

Contents

Contents, *continued*

COLOR PLATES

MAPS

Acknowledgements

This book was made possible through the combined efforts of a number of knowledgable and talented people. To Al Cohen, professor of Chinese in the Department of Asian Languages, University of Massachusetts at Amherst, we owe heartfelt gratitude for inspiration in the study of Chinese folk culture, generous photographic contributions, and helpful advice, comments, and criticisms on the manuscript. We would like to thank Po Sungnien, professor at the Central Academy of Fine Arts in Beijing and visiting professor at the University of California, Berkeley, in the Chinese Popular Culture Project for colorful New Year images, informative talks on New Year customs, and a Kitchen God to watch over Carol's hearth.

To photojournalist How Man Wong, we extend much appreciation for sharing his expertise on Chinese minorities and providing compelling images of festival happenings. For allowing an open-ended tour of their extensive photo archives of Western China, many thanks are due to Al Dien, professor of Chinese in the Department of Asian Languages, Stanford University, and to photographers Charlotte Temple and Regan Louie.

We are also grateful to Sue Gartley, project director of Folk Art International Resources for Education (FAIRE), for her warm support and for loaning useful resource materials as well as providing captivating images from FAIRE's photo archives by photographers Kim Raftery and Jonathan Fisher; to Terese Bartholomew, curator of Indian and Tibetan art at the Asian Art Museum of San Francisco, for materials in Chinese and helpful suggestions; and to Marijane Lee for sharing festival adventures and insights.

We owe a great debt to the talented art and design team of Robbin Henderson, Linda Revel, and Wendy Lee. Thanks also to Nancy Ippolito, China Books book division manager, and to the gifted young interns at China Books, Tim Farrell, Anna Lee, and Rachel Saidman.

We reserve special thanks to Bob Schildgen, whose skilled editorial work and guidance throughout the development of this book made this project a reality and a thoroughly enjoyable experience.

Special personal thanks to family, friends, and relatives for their encouragement and support throughout the writing. And lastly, to everyone who plays a part in the continuing art of celebration: keep the spirit!

Introduction

One of the Chinese words that comes to mind when you are watching or participating in Chinese festivals is *renao,* meaning "noisy, flourishing, lively and animated." It is used to describe the sensational and exciting aspects of celebrations and gatherings—the blazing color, the ear-splitting din, the long-awaited festival foods, the colorful street performances. There isn't any word in the English language that really comes close to the delightful sense of disorder and boisterousness which is a part of Chinese festivals.

Journeying from event to event, what we realized (as festival observers, participants, mythologists and anthropologists have through the ages) is that to experience a festival in all its fanfare and commotion, you are required to set aside all day-to-day worries and cares in favor of a mood of make-believe and masquerade. For a time—as in the primitive world of gods and demons where the festivals of today have their roots—we play the game of "as if," freeing our mind and spirit, dissolving the laws of time and space, standing on the borderline between belief and disbelief.

Throughout the year, people around the world reenact the rituals practiced by their parents, grandparents, and earlier ancestors. Whether it's Native American mountain spirit dancing or the lively costumed balls of the Mardi Gras, we still commemorate occasions in much the same way as in the ancient past through special costumes, makeup and ornamentation, enhancing the mood further by music, feasting, and sharing. Celebrations and festivals are necessary for society and for the individual—they are about cultural identity, life transitions, and personal discovery.

One of the best and most enjoyable ways to learn about a culture is by participating in its living festivals, and in pre–1949 China, and still in Hong Kong, Taiwan, and the overseas Chinese communities, festivals dominate the traditional calendar. Every month there are public festivals or domestic ceremonies, sensational birthday celebrations for the gods, or seasonal religious rites. These events may commemorate historical figures or mythical beings. In some cases, they are for the purpose of worshiping ancestors and deities. In other cases, they are for safeguarding the year and praying for prosperous times ahead. In all cases, holidays unite individuals by bringing families and friends together to celebrate and to share in their communal heritage and personal memories.

Although much of the same ambience and many of the same components—food, dance, fortunetelling, opera performances and processions—can be found in all festivals, each Chinese celebration has its own distinct trademark which stands out in the mind of the participant. For instance, the New Year is highlighted by lion dances and lantern parades; the Dragon Boat Festival draws crowds together for competitive boat races; the Mid-Autumn Festival inspires family gatherings to enjoy the moonlight; and on the Mounting the Heights Festival—celebrated by some families on the ninth day of the ninth moon (Double Ninth)—parents and children, friends and relatives climb mountains, enjoy looking at chrysanthemums, and fly kites.

Of course, since the Chinese have such a long historical tradition and China is an immense land with tremendous regional diversity as well as over 50 distinct minority ethnic groups, one cannot expect local customs to be exactly the same for each community. Like Fourth of July celebrations in the United States, one only has to travel from town to town to see different sets of parades, festival foods, and pyrotechnic displays. And, as we all know, the crowds drawn to the festivities are very diverse, with participants of all ages and from all levels of education and income.

Despite the local variations, a visit to Chinese temples and homes during a typical lunar year does reveal certain themes common to all festivals: the need to honor gods, ghosts, and ancestors. Indeed, the major Chinese festivals have a strong religious background, even though many are highly secularized today. Religious aspects of an event vary tremendously, but in the popular belief that is still alive in Hong Kong and Taiwan, homage to spiritual beings plays an important role in festivities.

In Chinese popular religion there's really no hard line between the sacred and the secular, or between this world and the invisible world of gods and ghosts. In fact, there's almost a kind of streetcorner accessibility to deities of the otherworld, whose images can be found everywhere from department stores and hilltop shrines to comic books and morality tracts.

The structure and day-to-day systems governing the world of spirits mirrors the real world in almost every way. The general assumption is that the deities, ancestors, and ghosts have essentially the same needs as the living. During festivals, people communicate with the unseeable portion of the world by offering the same things that are useful in real life—food, entertainment, and money. Because of the belief that the spiritual beings will reciprocate, worshipers ask for prosperity and moral direction for the individual, family, and community. The collection of religious practices surrounding the religion's tenets is called, simply enough, *baishen,* or "worshiping the deities," and is a unique blend of ancestor worship, animism, popular Taoist and Buddhist spiritual beliefs, and Confucian codes of ethics.

"Festivals for the Living," "Festivals for the Dead"

The reciprocity between spiritual beings and living people is reflected in the popular terminology used to describe the major Chinese festivals: "Festivals for the Living": (1) Lunar New Year, (2) Dragon Boat Festival, and (3) Mid-Autumn Festival, and "Festivals for the Dead": (1) Pure Brightness Festival and (2) Festival of Hungry Ghosts.

This book classifies the major festivals according to this traditional division, rather than following a month-by-month chronology, which is how most previous studies of Chinese festivals have been organized. For reference, however, a chronological listing of celebrations selected from the Chinese almanac *(Tong shu),* which is somewhat similar to the Farmer's Almanac, is included in the Appendix.

Thus, the first section focuses on beliefs and customs having to do with families and their relations with the gods, while the second section features the dark side of festival lore which is concerned more with the death and care of ancestors and uncared-for ghosts.

Because New Year is the most prominent and important of all Chinese holidays, rich with festival imagery and long-held traditions, it is discussed here in considerably greater detail than the other events. Besides chronicling the major seasonal celebrations and minor festive holidays, this compendium also looks at transition stages of life, in particular the wedding as celebrated in a traditional rural family. The nuances and variety of holiday celebrations are further revealed in a brief look at some of the unique festivals enjoyed by China's ethnic nationalities who occupy 50 to

60% of the land while comprising about one-twelfth of China's total population.

Among the ethnic minorities of China, the Miao, Yao, Tibetan, Mongol and Uygur peoples, for example, there are a great variety of festivities including burning torches, water splashing, moonlight dancing, bull-fighting, horse-racing, and wrestling.[1] Our selection of these minorities' festivals is rather limited because of space and because of the difficulties in exploring among these people. We can only hope that other adventurers to Asia will share their observations and educate us further about this very large and vital part of the Asian continent.

Much of the material in this book stems from the authors' and photographers' stays in China, Taiwan, and Hong Kong as well as their first-hand experiences in San Francisco's Chinatown. A great deal more, however, has also been gleaned from researching the available literature, some of which consists of rare or out-of-print sources now difficult to obtain. Especially helpful are those publications with a regional focus—for instance, Lewis Hodous' *Folkways in China* (Fujian Province) or Joan Law and Barbara Ward's *Chinese Festivals* (Hong Kong). There's also Wolfram Eberhard's *Local Cultures in Ancient China* and *Chinese Festivals,* which are essential reading for anyone concerned with the subject of festivals. Compiled by one of the leading sinologists in the field, these two works contain references to historical narratives, dynastic histories, and specialized works on festivals.

Unfortunately, there is very little in translation about Chinese life and customs as the Chinese themselves regard them. One of the most helpful contributions in this area is Derk Bodde's translation of the *Yenjing suishiji* (Record of Yearly Events at Yenjing [Beijing]) written at the turn of this century by Dun Lichen, a Manchurian from a noble family in China. These sources and those listed in the bibliography will make fascinating additional reading for anyone wanting to learn more about Chinese popular thought and culture.

Throughout the ages and clearly into modern times, festivals have continued to enjoy immense popularity. As to whether the celebrations as they are traditionally characterized will continue to flourish or slowly disappear, it's difficult to speculate. Festivals, after all, are living, dynamic celebrations and there have been significant changes in them over time in all cultures, especially in the last hundred years. Part of the change is a growing "secularization" of society as it is affected by modern ideas, and part of the change is reflected in a burgeoning tourist industry. Economics determine to some extent what is enacted on a festival day.

Yet traditional festival practices are still widely observed, even in such cosmopolitan places as Hong Kong and Taiwan. Authors Joan Law and Barbara Ward have cited accounts of temple fairs in Guangdong Province in the 1860s that describe in almost every way what can be seen in Hong Kong today. Perhaps the entire long tradition survives because of its flexibility and lack of dogma, which allow the opportunity for local innovations and individual devotional practices.[2]

The situation is different in the People's Republic of China. Many religious festival activities were officially discouraged or forbidden after the establishment of the People's Republic in 1949. However, after a long period of hibernation, various spiritual and magico-religious practices are resurfacing. According to some China watchers, it is only a matter of time before many old traditions will regain acceptance. This is especially true of those rural areas where many traditions never completely vanished.[3]

Finally, in overseas Chinese communities like San Francisco's or New York's Chinatowns, certain festivals are celebrated with great enthusiasm, such as the Chinese Lunar New Year. Everyone takes to the street for the annual New Year parade. In San Francisco, this is an almost 40-year-old tradition featuring prancing dragons and politicos, beauties, bands and lion dancers. Although many Chinese-Americans no longer follow all of the elaborate customs associated with lunar New Year festivities, they still see it as a time for reckoning with the past and resolving old debts and hurts. It is a time to gather the family together as a source of support, energy, and continuity.

In fact, it is this sense of family unity and harmony called *yuan* in Chinese that truly underlies all Chinese festivals. *Yuan,* "roundness," suggests the attainment of what are commonly known as the Five Happinesses: long life, wealth, peace, virtue, and honor. Roundness suggests a unity of the family circle and a unity of society. In essence, the symbols, stories, and entertainment, taken in their most basic forms, are colorful motifs to ensure the timeless wishes of harmony and goodwill. This is perhaps the most vital concept to remember as you delve into the diversity and range of Chinese festivals described in the pages ahead.

A Note on Pronunciation of Chinese Words

The *pinyin* romanization system is used throughout this book. The official system of the People's Republic of China and the system adopted by most U.S. newspapers and magazines, it is one of the easiest romanizations to learn, with fewer letters per sound than any other system. Most of the pronunciations are easily identifiable for non-Chinese speakers, with the following exceptions:

c is pronounced like *ts,* as in "bats"
zh is like *j,* as in "jump"
q is like *ch,* as in "chew"
x is like *sh,* as in "shoe"

FESTIVALS OF THE LIVING

The New Year Festival
(1st day, 1st moon)
Xin Nian

The most colorful, sensational, and joyous of all Chinese festivals is the Lunar New Year. Everywhere in China and overseas, Chinese communities and families prepare for a series of celebratory events that can last anywhere from one to three days to two weeks.

During festival time, marketplaces are bursting with color— plum blossoms, red azaleas, oranges, and tangerines fill streetside stalls. Sidewalk tables are covered with bright red paper couplets expressing good fortune, window decorations, lunar calendars, and almanacs. Whole roast pigs are on display in restaurant windows, and candied kumquats, lotus nuts, and melon seeds are available in grocery stores for the eight-sided Tray of Togetherness.

As the New Year festivities progress, people inside giant colorful lion and dragon masks dance through the streets to the sound of explod- ing firecrackers, the rhythmic beat of drums, and the loud crashing of cymbals. At this time of year more than any other, the primary concerns of family, friends, and relatives are to ensure good luck, pay respects to the gods and spirits, and wish good fortune for the coming year.

The New Year of the Chinese lunar calendar is a movable feast, usually falling somewhere between January 21 and February 19, depending on what date the new moon appears. In their day-to-day lives, the Chinese treat January 1 as the official New Year's Day, following the Gregorian calendar. Their traditional New Year celebrations, however, continue to follow the lunar calendar, beginning with the new moon, which marks the first day of the first lunar month, and ending on the 15th day with the brilliant lights of the Lantern Festival. Still, there are exceptions—some New Year events don't coincide with the first day of the lunar month or even the first of January. And the Yi people, for example, one of China's ethnic minorities, celebrate the New Year in the 10th lunar month. There are no hard and fast rules as to when a particular event occurs—the timing differs from place to place as do particular customs. One should just bear in mind that the New Year is really a multi-layered festival with many local variations, but that each distinct aspect celebrates the common idea of a new beginning. *(For further discussion of the calendar system itself, see the Appendix.)*

The End of the Year: Some Thoughts on the Calendar

Even the sky seems to proclaim the arrival of the New Year, as the old calendar scrolls toward the last page, to say nothing of the villages and towns lying expectantly underneath. Pallid clouds loom overhead, intermittently brightened by flashes of firecrackers set off to bid farewell to the Hearth God. Faint whiffs of gunpowder already fill the air before the ears can recover from the ringing echoes of the deafening bangs.

—THE NEW YEAR SACRIFICE, by Lu Xun (1881–1936) (translated by the authors)

AND PROTECTION

, Welcoming in the New

opportunity to send away the
nd to prepare for starting afresh.
ng forces become dominant and
away. There is much to be done in
; with pasting up colorful New Year
pictures of door gods, and red luck-
with auspicious imagery. Sacrifices
of Buddha is cleansed, and the Soup
of the Eighth Day

Each day is filled with anticipation, imbued with both a sense of
spiritual protection and boisterousness, and colored with symbolism,
offering people what they long for most: happiness, riches, and good
health.

Soup of the Eighth Day

Prior to the New Year, on the 8th day of the 12th month, everyone cooks
the "Soup of the Eighth Day," or *labazhou*. The word *la,* meaning "together," is the name of an ancient Chinese ceremony that took place shortly
after the winter solstice. Sacrifices were made to all spiritual powers—
heaven and earth as well as one's deities and ancestors. Accounts from the
Southern Song dynasty (1127–1279) record villagers on the 8th day of the
12th moon beating waist drums and wearing masks to disguise themselves
as the Buddhist deity Vajra for the purpose of chasing out epidemics and
averting disaster.[1] The day of *laba* marked the interval between the
outgoing year and the incoming year, and its customs and practices
culminated in a festival of exorcism, renewal, and thanksgiving.

Laba Gruel

Laba gruel is a very thick porridge that resembles mince pie or plum
pudding. It consists of various whole grains and/or rice topped with dried

fruits and nuts such as dates, chestnuts, pine seeds, and raisins.

As to the origin of *laba,* there are several interesting legends. One story attributes its creation to Sakyamuni, an Indian prince of the sixth century B.C., who left the luxurious comfort of his home, attained enlightenment, and thenceforth was known as the Buddha. His teachings started to gain strong influence in China as early as the second and third centuries A.D. Buddhism's pantheon of compassionate saints, its emphasis on meditation, and its belief in tolerance and piety captured the religious mind of the Chinese, and along with Taoism and Confucianism it became one of the three doctrines of China. If Sakyamuni's austere life as a wandering teacher is in some respects like Christ's, then *laba* could be considered a type of eucharist. On his journeys Sakyamuni ate meager servings of grains and vegetables, so to remember Sakyamuni's hardship, his disciples (whose roles and characters even have parallels with Christ's disciples) consumed a type of porridge consisting of beans, fruit and barley on the eighth day of the 12th month—the day Sakyamuni achieved enlightenment. This porridge is made at the break of dawn at all the major Buddhist temples, and monks believe that by consuming it they will be protected by the spirit of Buddha.

Another version of *laba's* origin recounts Sakyamuni's arduous journeys through mountains and rivers until, after days of traveling without rest, he collapsed near a river in northern India. He was revived by a wandering shepherdess, who offered him her lunch of family leftovers consisting of sticky cereal, glutinous rice, dates, chestnuts, and wild fruit. After consuming this repast, Sakyamuni took a bath and sat under a tree for meditation where he finally attained enlightenment. This meal was the original *laba*.

Still another legend describes nothing of Buddhist origins, but tells instead of a type of *laba* made by a poor mother whose unfilial son drove her to beg from the neighbors. The hungry woman received a mixture of fruits and beans from sympathetic friends that set the standard for the type of *laba* still widely consumed today, especially in northern parts of China.

Sakyamuni as an ascetic (jade carving from Qing dynasty; courtesy of Asian Art Museum, San Francisco).

Customs and History

Folk tradition dates the preparation of *labazhou* as far back as the Han dynasty (206 B.C.–A.D. 220). The custom of eating the porridge became especially widespread during the Tang dynasty (618–906), when Buddhism had already come of age in China and the Buddhists had fully incorporated the consumption of *labazhou* into their remembrance feast for Sakyamuni. By the Qing dynasty (1644–1911) cooking *laba* was a standard custom in the kitchens of the imperial court, Buddhist monasteries, and village homes. During the Kangxi reign (1662–1722), the emperor bestowed this special dish as a gift to ministers, officers, and abbots of leading monasteries. Eunuchs also distributed the *laba* to households throughout the empire, receiving in return lavish gifts.

At the same time, families distributed the gruel to relatives and friends after first making a dedication to Buddha, often presenting *laba* with an accompanying dish, usually of pickled cabbage. The cabbage was carefully cultivated in shallow pits or root cellars and its delicate and tender shoots were considered of incomparable quality. It was said that the future prosperity or decline of the household could be predicted according to whether they turned out sweet or sour.

Beijing-Style *Laba*

Laba varies considerably from province to province. In the North it is salty, in the South it is sweet. Some epicureans consider Beijing-style *laba* the most authentic since Beijing's culinary traditions span five dynasties of imperial cooking.

The basic recipe uses at least five grains—millet, maize, sorghum, glutinous rice, and barley—as well as red beans. An assortment of dried fruits is added to the simmering grain mixture, the most important being jujube or red dates. The dates are skinned and pitted, with the skins being used to make an exceptionally piquant broth that is later poured into the soup. Next, dried lily and lotus seeds are tossed in, with the remaining ingredients—dates, chestnuts, and pine seeds—added at the very end.

Hazelnuts, almonds and walnuts used as toppings are soaked in sugar water before serving to prevent them from drying out. To sweeten the *laba*, brown sugar (not white sugar) may be added. It is customary to sip the *laba* from individual bowls. No utensils are required for eating this simple but wholesome and nutritious meal.

If the cooked *laba* is not eaten all at once, the remaining porridge can be poured into jars and stored without refrigeration in unheated pantries. The frigid winter climate of the North solidifies the *laba* and prevents any spoilage, and all one has to do to make a meal of *laba* is to slice a chunk off and warm it up.

SENDING OFF THE KITCHEN GOD

Ascend to Heaven and speak of good things;
Send blessings down to the world below . . .

A kitchen stove in a typical Chinese country home (Beijing).

Stoves

The standing mud-covered brick stoves in a traditional Chinese kitchen are huge. They are built up from the floor against a wall of the kitchen and look something like altars and, in fact, they are. The family stove, apart from its functional importance, was believed to house the Kitchen God, also called the Lord of the Hearth (Zao Jun), one of the oldest gods worshiped in China. (The Kitchen God has a little niche behind the cooking stove for incense and offerings, but his special center of interest is regarded as the hearth itself.)

The stove is considered the soul of the family. In sociological terms, the stove identifies a family as a cohesive entity and represents its corporate fate. In diviner's terms, good stoves will guarantee peace in the family, while bad ones bring strife.[2]

Kitchen God Ascends to Heaven

Within the bureaucratic pantheon in Heaven, the Kitchen God acts as a minor guardian, much like the neighborhood Earth God (Tudigong). But, whereas the Earth God governs an entire community, the Kitchen God is identified with a single family. To further explain the difference, some claim that the Earth God acts something like a policeman who reports to the provincial City God, while the Kitchen God performs more like a plain-clothesman who reports to the highest spiritual being, the Jade Emperor (Yuhuangdi).

Folk print of the Kitchen God and his wife.

As an agent of heavenly authority, the Kitchen God spends the whole year with the family, seeing and hearing everything. Once a year, on the 23d of the last month of the lunar year (the 24th in the South), he ascends to heaven to make his annual report. At this time, commonly called the "Little New Year" *(xiaonian),* the family gives him a farewell dinner with offerings of sweet cakes and preserved fruits. In some areas of China, the deity's mouth is smeared with honey or sticky rice. This is so he will say only sweet things, or, according to some, because it makes his mouth so sticky he will not be able to utter a single word.

Next, a woodblock print with the god's image on it, along with a horse made of paper (in some cases sorghum stem), is set on fire. The burning of the image releases the god for his "ascent" to heaven. As the Kitchen God soars to heaven on his steed, paper spirit money (called *qianchang* or *yuanbao*) is thrown into the fire along with straw for the horse. Peas and beans are tossed onto the roof to symbolize the clatter of the horse's hooves.

In most prints the Kitchen God, wearing the robes and hat of a noble magistrate, is seated next to his wife and attended by several immortal lads and maidens. Vases and flowers surround the Kitchen God's offering table and usually there is space on the upper portion of the print for a calendar. Sometimes a rooster and a dog are also pictured as domestic symbols of a rural household. Although the style and imagery of the prints vary from locality to locality, certain aspects are the same—everywhere the Kitchen God is depicted as a compassionate deity associated with the warmth of the hearth, family, and good fortune.

Worshiping the Kitchen God (contemporary Chinese folk painting).

Master of the Household

As a Taiwanese temple keeper put it in an interview, the Kitchen God is considered to play a crucial role in "rewarding good, dispersing calamity and accumulating good fortune, admonishing the world and enlightening the people."[3] For members of the household this means that since he keeps the domestic register, he is the one who determines the fortune of the family. He is honored as "master of the household" *(yichia zhizhu)*.

There are a great number of legends about the origin of the Kitchen God. A story popular in south and central China tells of a poor mason destined to remain penniless all his life. The hard-working but luckless man was unable to support his wife and therefore the couple eventually had to separate. Many years later, the mason went to work for his former wife's new and prosperous family. The wife, whom he did not recognize, hid a few pieces of gold in the sesame cakes she made for his journey home. Unfortunately, he sold the cakes and never found the gold. When he later discovered the truth about the cakes, he became despondent and ended his own life. Upon hearing this sad story, the Jade Emperor made the mason God of the Hearth for his goodness and honesty.[4]

According to another tale, the human deified as Kitchen God (whose historical family, the Zhang, is described in the Tang dynasty compendium, *Youyang Miscellanies*) didn't possess any virtuous characteristics, but was a spendthrift who deserted his wife for a young and lazy concubine. He squandered his entire fortune on her, and the concubine eventually married someone else while Zhang begged for food throughout the countryside. One cold winter day a kindhearted widow gave him food, clothing and shelter. When Zhang recognized this woman as his former wife, he felt so ashamed that he crawled into the kitchen stove in an effort to hide himself and was burned to ashes. His ex-wife, realizing he was her first husband, died from grief a few days later. Since Zhang admitted his wrongdoing in the end, he was deified as the Kitchen God and his wife became the Kitchen Goddess.

Today, sending off the Kitchen God is still a favorite custom and one that has been observed in the People's Republic of China despite official edicts prohibiting the hanging of his picture over the hearthplace.

SEQUENCE OF TRADITIONAL NEW YEAR EVENTS

MOON 12

DAY 8

Offering of *labazhou*.

DAY 23 OR 24

Kitchen God ascends to Heaven.

DAY 30

New Year's Eve. Offerings to gods and ancestors are made, family reunion meal takes place, elders distribute "money of the passing year"; everyone stays awake to safeguard the year; family members paste spring scrolls on doorways and gates.

MOON 1

DAY 1

New Year's Day. Pay respects to elders, set off firecrackers, burn incense and worship deities; call on friends and relatives.

DAYS 1–5

Beginning of New Spring. Worship the God of Wealth; married women visit natal homes, sweep houses to send off poverty, keep an open house for visiting friends and relatives; temple astrologers predict fortunes.

DAY 7

Birthday of Humanity. The first 10 days of the New Year are dedicated to animals, foods, and humans; the first, the day of fowl; the second, of dogs; the third, pigs; the fourth, ducks; fifth, oxen; sixth, horses; seventh, humanity; eighth, rice; ninth, fruit and vegetables; tenth, wheat and barley.

DAY 15

The Lantern Festival Day. Parades in San Francisco and other major cities are set as close to this date as possible.

DOOR GODS, NEW YEAR PRINTS, AND SPRING COUPLETS

On the last day of the 12th moon, gate posts and door panels are brilliantly decorated with door gods *(menshen)* and luck-bringing papers or "spring couplets" *(chunlian)*. This popular custom originated more than one thousand years ago when peachwood charms were hung on the main gates of households.

Door Gods

Often carved or painted on ancient charms were images of two gods, Shentu and Yulu, guardians of the underworld who protected families from demons by seizing the demons, binding them with reed ropes, and throwing them to their tigers in the shadowy depths of the nether regions. These images have been chronicled as far back as the late second century A.D. and are the earliest evidence of what can be called New Year pictures.

Such fierce protectors of the gate are depicted in full armor, brandishing swords and weapons, ready to attack. Contemporary prints show faces of the door gods painted with the vibrant make-up *(lianpu)* of Chinese opera—their poses, costumes and weapons also reflecting the influence of local theater. [See color plate 2a.]

Tamer gods or civilian officers wearing officials' caps and long-sleeved robes were developed in Song dynasty times (960–1279) and later paired with their martial counterparts to represent the civil and military realms of government. (This is a division characteristic of Chinese governmental structure that goes back to archaic times.)

Door gods remained popular over the centuries, and from the 12th through the 13th centuries, with the practice of printing from woodblocks widely in use, their images were sold in great number during the New Year festival. There were many types of guardians of the main gate, including roosters and tigers, but especially popular to this day are the Tang dynasty generals Qin Qiong (also known as Qin Shubao) and Yuchi Jingde (also known as Hu Jingde). The origin of these door gods is associated with the famous Tang dynasty emperor Tai Zong, who was plagued in his sleep by evil demons:

> "Believe me or not," said the Emperor, "as soon as night comes on, bricks and tiles hurtle about just outside my room, and ghosts or goblins scream in a manner truly terrible. If it were in the daytime, I could make shift to put up with it, but on my dark nights it is unendurable." "Your majesty need not be disquieted," said the minister Ch'in Shu-pao [Qin Shubao]. "I and my colleague Hu Ching-te [Hu Jingde] will tonight mount guard outside the palace gates, and will find out what spirit it is that is haunting you." The offer was accepted, and the two ministers, in full armour and axe in hand, took up their position outside the palace gates. But dawn came without the slightest sign of any apparition. The Emperor had a good night's rest, and in the morning sent handsome rewards to the two watchers. The same precaution was taken for several nights in succession, with the same result . . . At the end of this period, the Emperor sent for the two ministers and said that he could not bear the idea of their being put to this inconvenience any longer. "I shall send for a clever painter," he said, "to make your portraits and fasten them up on each side of the gate. Would that not be a good plan?" The ministers accordingly dressed up in armour, and posed for the painter. Their portraits were fastened up on the gate, and nothing happened all night.
>
> —MONKEY (translated by Arthur Waley)

Spring Couplets

While pairs of door gods are pasted in the center panels of doors, spring couplets are pasted on each side of the front door and propitious words across the lintel at the top. In old China, scholars accomplished in the art of writing would set up the tools of their trade in their studio—brush, ink, inkstone and paper—and compose auspicious couplets for friends, relatives and the public at large.

A calligrapher would prepare to write by first grinding the dry ink with water on an inkstone. Dipping into the rich, black mixture, he would

Spring couplets and papercuts displayed at a New Year fair (Beijing).

masterfully move the brush over paper to produce powerful, clean strokes, forming elegant characters with well-jointed turns and hooks in a variety of styles—cursive, running, or standard. The themes of the verses would suggest good fortune, longevity and, traditionally, male offspring.

Today, calligraphers still hand write spring couplets, but they are more commonly sold commercially, mass-produced on modern printing presses like greeting cards. Printed on red paper about a foot long with characters embossed in gold ink, couplets and good luck characters can be readily purchased at stationery stores, book stores and magazine stands wherever there is a substantial Chinese population.

The first couplets composed specifically to bring good fortune and not simply extracted from verse are attributed to Emperor Meng Zhang in the 10th century. Not pleased with the literary attempts of his court scholars, he composed his own couplet to decorate his bedchamber door:

The New Year brings in overflowing good fortune,
The great festival is named Everlasting Spring.

This was probably the first New Year couplet used as adornment for a part of a building.

It wasn't until the Ming dynasty (1368–1644) that spring couplets came into style for everyone—officials, scholars, and commoners alike. During the Qing dynasty (1644–1911), the composition of couplets became a way of measuring one's literary talent. An individual's education and wit were tested by how well he could match a given line of a couplet.

Although the requirements for composing a couplet are simple enough, the art of antithetical writing is still a challenge. A couplet is made up of two lines of verse which are called the "head" and "tail" respectively and which should correspond with each other phonologically and syntactically word for word and phrase for phrase. In past times, children were given exercises in which they practiced couplet-writing by first setting single words against each other, then gradually moving up the ladder to two-character, three-character, five-character, and seven-character combinations.

An example of antithetical pairing is the following verse:

By virtue united, heaven is strong (de he gan geng)

Through compassion shared, earth is yielding
(ci tong kun shun).

Here the words "virtue" and "compassion" are both nouns of the same category, as are "heaven" and "earth"; the words "united" and "shared" are both passive verbs; the words "strong" and "yielding" structurally serve the same purpose while being opposite in meaning.

The brevity and concentrated meaning of the couplet is uniquely Chinese. It leaves out more than it says and, through the visual quality of characters, reveals a hidden dimension which readers have to puzzle out themselves.

This custom has not been discouraged by communist ideologies, and in fact has given rise to a whole new set of popular expressions. The content of contemporary New Year couplets from the People's Republic of China often sets political terminology against traditional descriptive elements. For example, "red flags" might be paired with "fresh flowers." The emphasis on social work ethics and collective virtues is typically found in phrases that couple "people's communes are prospering" with "socialism is flourishing" or "uphold the glorious traditions of our Party" with "preserve the spirit of the working people."[5]

There is less political ideology in couplets from Taiwan and a greater emphasis on wealth and profit, as might be expected from a society that strongly encourages private enterprise. The traditional New Year wish for money and success in business takes on global dimensions in parallel combinations such as:

Our business reputation is known throughout 10,000
countries,
Our branch offices are established on 5 continents.[6]

Not all luck-bringing papers are couplets. Some are four-character phrases that express traditional sentiments for a rich and bountiful spring. Still others are single characters, for example, the word for "blessings/good fortune," *fu.* It is often pasted upside down because the word for "upside down" sounds the same as the word "to arrive." The upside down *fu* becomes a pun that implies "good fortune has arrived!" [See color plate 2c.]

The Color Red and the Festival Mood

The cheerful bright red couplets and papercuts, complemented by plates of oranges, red *hong-bao* envelopes, and red luck candies that are displayed in homes, offices, and businesses during the New Year, immediately convey a festive mood of joy and good tidings. Aside from being an auspicious color, however, red was also once painted on doorways to frighten away demons.

As with so many other common elements of Chinese culture, there is a story to explain how the color red became so popular and powerful. In ancient times, according to legend, there was a horrible creature called *nian* (the same as the word for "year" itself) that appeared at the end of the year. The beast attacked the people and their livestock, and even though the villagers fought fiercely together, they never succeeded in destroying the creature.

After many failures, the villagers discovered the *nian* monster had three weaknesses—it was frightened by noise, it disliked sunshine, and it was terrified of the color red. So, at the end of the year, the people built a huge bonfire outside the village, set off hundreds of firecrackers and painted the doors of their homes red. Upon seeing the commotion, the *nian* monster became so panicked that it covered its head in fear and ran away. And this is how, some say, that bright red became the color of the New Year.

Transporting bundles of firecrackers on bicycles (Beijing).

New Year Prints

Folk print of "one hundred sons" at play.

Some of the most striking images posted at the same time as door gods and spring couplets are New Year prints *(nianhua),* which visually depict through plant and animal symbols what the couplets so poetically describe. Wishes for riches and honor are represented by full-blossomed peonies, and the desire for many children is suggested by many-seeded pomegranates. Auspicious rebuses are composed with such motifs as the deer and the bat, homonyms respectively for "high position" *(lu)* and "good fortune" *(fu).*

The colors are bright, intense and explosive *(bao).* The sharpness of the hues is referred to as *jian,* its fieriness and glare as *yang.*

The types of *nianhua* range from religious images of deities, or "horse sheets" *(mazhang),* that are pasted up and then burned as sacrifices, to scenes of everyday events—pictures of men and women at work known as "plowing and weaving" prints *(gengzhitu).* There are also numerous symbolic figures and objects such as peaches (representing longevity) and plump and healthy children holding gold coins and pots of treasure (representing progeny and wealth). Another popular theme during the New Year is the "One Hundred Sons" or *baizitu* prints showing young boys romping together, flying kites, playing instruments, or carrying dragon lanterns. Finally, there are scenes from historical novels and popular operas, the old Chinese novels *Journey to the West* and *Romance of the Three Kingdoms* being favorite sources for such New Year art and entertainment.[7]

As might be expected in the People's Republic of China, the style and subject matter changed with the times. There was a demand for art with political content or a socialist theme. The routine peasant style characterized by black contour lines, bright colors and informal compositional techniques was replaced by one that was highly representational. Socialist

An entire wall covered with New Year prints (Beijing).

Realist art from the Soviet Union and Chinese brush painting combined with Western perspective devices and chiaroscuro, to provide the models for contemporary folk prints and painting.[8]

The new subject matter was infused with new themes focusing on such topics as cooperative labor and bumper harvests. Woodblock prints, following the development of amateur and professional Chinese peasant painting, began to include pictures of corn harvests and spring hoeing. Thus, instead of a scene depicting the traditional wish of five sons achieving success in the civil service examinations, the contemporary counterpart was a picture of a bumper harvest of the five principal cereals.

Since the end of the Cultural Revolution (1966–1976), there has been a greater receptivity to traditional styles. Although New Year themes mirror the new political reality, auspicious sentiments for the New Year still prevail. For example, while a picture depicting the communal fish pond supports government aquaculture, it also symbolizes the traditional New Year hope for abundance (since the word for "fish" is a homonym of the word for "abundance").

As for the production and sale of New Year prints, historically famous places were Taohuawu in southern China (Suzhou) and Yangliuqing in northern China (Tianjin), both of which can trace their traditions back to the 17th century. Suzhou in particular was important as a major center in the development of color woodblock printing. Other important *nianhua* centers were Weifang in Shandong Province, Mianzhu in Sichuan Province, and Foshan in Guangdong Province. At the turn of the century, during the peak of production at Yanliuqing, up to a million prints a year were produced. Today, *nianhua* workshops throughout China produce a total of more than a hundred million New Year prints in a single year.[9]

New Year festival portrayed in a classical Chinese print.

FAMILY AND FOOD
A Time of Reunion and Celebration

New Year's Eve and New Year's Day are celebrated as a family affair, a time of reunion and thanksgiving. The celebration was traditionally highlighted with a religious ceremony given in honor of Heaven and Earth, the gods of the household, and the family ancestors. The head of each household presents incense, flowers, food and wine to ensure continued blessings and good fortune.

The sacrifice to the ancestors, the most vital of all the rituals, united the living members with those who had passed away. Departed relatives were remembered with great respect in the past as they still are today because they were responsible for laying the foundations for the fortune and glory of the family.

The presence of the ancestors is acknowledged on the eve of the New Year with a dinner setting arranged for them at the family banquet table. The spirits of the ancestors, together with the living, celebrate the onset of the New Year as one great community. The communal feast called "surrounding the stove" *(weilu)* symbolizes the unity of the family and honors the past and present generations of the lineage.

Such celebratory occasions were greatly missed by many early Chinese immigrants to the United States, the majority of whom were single men. For many, clan associations (a type of social club or lodge) functioned as a substitute for family, and in place of family banquets, clan associations developed a tradition of spring banquets. Today, spring banquets are still held at restaurants in major Chinese communities such as San Francisco's Chinatown, although such gatherings are now attended by several generations of families, with husbands and wives, children and grandchildren, all assembled together at one table.

Auspicious Foods

At these affairs and throughout New Year's Day, everyone peppers their speech with words and phrases suggesting auspicious things. No unpleasant words or thoughts are permitted to be spoken. This idea is carried through to the reunion meal where every dish has a name which symbolizes in some way health, honor, and riches. One specialty served is called "Broth of Prosperity," a chicken soup filled with "gold and silver ingots" (egg dumplings and pigeon eggs). Seasoned pork shoulder is called "Mist of Harmony." A combination of sea cucumber, squid and seaweed is named "Jade of Ink, Gold of Darkness." Thin, semi-transparent strands of bean vermicelli are referred to as "silvery threads of longevity," platters of chicken wings imply "to soar one thousand miles," and dishes of pigs' trotters invite the diner to "tread the azure clouds of good fortune."

Winter bamboo shoots, because they grow so tall, suggest the phrase "year after year, ascend to great heights." Giant pork meatballs, or "lions' heads," and hard-boiled eggs (one for each member of the family) symbolize happy reunion because of their round shape. Chicken or fish is served whole with head and tail to suggest "a favorable start and finish."

After the feasting is over, parents give their children small red envelopes *(hongbao)* that contain "lucky" money. This is called "money of the year that is given away" *(yasuiqian)*.

Jiaozi

Another popular New Year dish made in family kitchens throughout northern China are small meat dumplings called *jiaozi*. Wrapped in a thin layer of dough, the filling consists of chopped pork and cabbage, ginger, shrimp, black mushrooms, scallions, garlic, and ground pepper. Some portion of the hundreds of dumplings made in a single household were traditionally stuffed with copper coins, pieces of gold and silver, or even precious stones to suggest a prosperous year ahead. Edible surprise fillings included peanuts because the words for "peanut" *(sheng)* and "life" *(sheng)* are homonyms. In addition, dates *(zao)* and chestnuts *(lizi)* were considered auspicious since the combined words for these nuts sound like "early son" *(zaozi)*.

Street-corner vendor selling New Year food (Beijing).

To cook *jiaozi,* the chef drops them in a large pot of boiling water for a couple of minutes, then removes the pot from the heat and leaves the *jiaozi* in the water for about 15 minutes. If they are pan-fried, the dish is called "pot stickers" *(guotie)*. Both styles of dumplings are eaten with a variety of communal dipping sauces such as soy sauce, vinegar, chili bean sauce, or chili oil.

Fruits and Nuts

For the next few days a steady stream of friends and relatives visits the home, and a number of sumptuous meals are prepared. Before guests sample the main dishes, however, a variety of snacks in the form of fruits, nuts, and seeds are first offered. Almonds, sliced red dates, hazelnuts, red bay berries, pomegranate seeds, pears, apples, candied tangerines, honeyed jujubes, peaches and apricots—all these convey wishes for fertility and long life.

Some of the more popular candied delicacies are presented in an eight-sided tray called "The Tray of Togetherness" *(henian quanhe)*. Each of the items displayed invokes good fortune. For example, kumquats symbolize prosperity because the first Chinese written character for "kumquats" means "gold," while coconuts will promote togetherness. The Chinese word for lotus seeds sounds like the words for "many children," and the word for "lotus beans" suggests a full wallet. All of these snacks are economical, distinctive and special, making a tasty contribution to the feasts of the New Year.

New Year fruits: grapes, pomegranate, persimmon, watermelon, winter melon, hand citron, peaches, and pumpkin.

Guest Foods

After enjoying the array of preserved sweets, friends and relatives are invited to sample some of the specially prepared guest foods.

Of all the food staples for the New Year festival, wild game is indispensable. Families living in rural areas often prepare such delicious courses as pheasant stewed with fermented melon or wild rabbit soaked with five-spice sauce. Accompanied by a hearty red wine, these meat dishes make excellent holiday entrees. Other favorite New Year courses that are at once rich and not too greasy include fried white fish, stewed pork stomach, and crispy golden carp with scallions.

Additionally, Guangzhou (Canton) sausage and cured meat (which must be cooked, usually by steaming), and Hunan pork stewed with dried fish can also be served. If families are in a particularly festive mood, they can prepare these delicacies themselves, or buy a portion from stores specializing in the foods of Guangzhou and Hunan, a whole month in advance. In the cold climates of North China, sausages are hung outside under the edge of the roof to dry. During the frigid winter season, there is little concern about spoilage.

Around New Year's time, another essential dish for the holiday table is stir-fried salty vegetables. Southerners refer to this dish as "the plate of 10 fragrances," which probably should be interpreted as a combination of at least 10 different kinds of vegetables. Indeed, the number is often even higher.

The main ingredient is yellow bean sprouts, which are probably chosen because of the sprouts' resemblance to a certain kind of jade ornament signifying good luck. They are combined with carrots, dried lily buds ("golden needles"), black mushrooms, dried bean curd, salted ginger, winter mushrooms, and salted mustard leaves.

To make this dish, carrots are cut into thin slices and partially fried. The carrots are set aside, and then the bean sprouts are cooked along with the other ingredients (which have been cut ahead of time into thin slices). Next, the carrots are mixed with light soy sauce, salt, sugar, and cooking wine, and combined with the vegetables. In the South, hot pickled tubers and celery are added. Simple as the method may be, tastes vary tremendously from region to region. The key to success is that whatever dried or fresh vegetables are used, they must be sliced thinly and evenly so that the sauce can completely permeate the ingredients.

Crispy fish makes an excellent appetizer with dumplings and wine. It is made with fresh, whole small- to medium-sized golden carp. Four or five carp are optimal for one serving. After cleaning and scaling, the fish is marinated in soy sauce, rice vinegar, cooking wine and sugar for about 40 minutes. There should be enough sauce to cover the entire serving. The fish are fried in hot oil in a heated wok and then set aside. Next, in a separate pot, a thick layer of scallions and sliced ginger is used to cover each of the fish, which which are then stacked in layers like pancakes. The marinade used earlier is poured over the assemblage which is then cooked over medium heat for about an hour and a half. When the dish is ready to be served, a few drops of sesame oil are sprinkled over the top of the fish. It is preferred when served cold.

As ordinary as "shrimp paste" sounds, it takes a master to achieve the real flavor of this dish. Baby shrimp (which have been cleaned and shelled), together with a small portion of thinly sliced lean meat (pork or beef) are fried with scallions and ginger. This mixture is then combined with sliced winter bamboo shoots and fried with heavy Chinese bean paste.

(Beancurd, peanuts or sweet sauce should not be used as additional ingredients or substitutes.) Chinese hot sauce is an optional garnish to produce what food lovers from Shanghai refer to as "eight-jewel hot sauce."

During the New Year in cold climates like Beijing, cabbage that has been preserved in root cellars is sweet in taste and crunchy in texture. Easily prepared, steamed cabbage can make an excellent side dish for New Year *jiaozi* with a dipping sauce of heavy vinegar. To make this recipe, cabbage hearts are first soaked in water and cut diagonally, then covered with a sauce of Chinese mustard, sugar, and vinegar, and steamed until tender.

Popular novels such as *The Golden Lotus* (Jin ping mai) provide numerous descriptions of food in a variety of activities during the Ming dynasty (1368–1644). According to this novel, some of the delicacies typically enjoyed by the merchant class during the New Year season might include pork, ice-fish (*salanx cuvieri*) and steamed shortbreads with fruit and vegetable fillings. Exchange of food and gifts with nearby temples could be especially elaborate, depending on one's relationship with the head priest. Offerings might include as much as "ten catties of official candles, five catties of incense, two rolls of brocade, two jars of southern wine, four live geese, four live chickens, a set of pig's trotters, a leg of mutton and ten taels of silver." [10]

Niangao

In South China, during the New Year, there are many sweet pastries to try (more so than in the North). Sweet pastries are not normally consumed in the traditional Chinese diet, but they are considered special treats for festive occasions. Small sweets—which are easy to make and inexpensive—make a holiday memorable, especially for children who eagerly look forward to such mouth-watering edibles as nine-layer cake, fried dough, or date-filled pastry.

The most popular New Year dessert is *niangao,* a sweet steamed glutinous rice pudding. When people eat this dish, they preface their first bite with the phrase "promotion step by step" *(bubu denggao)* because the word for cake also sounds like the word for "soaring high." Like *jiaozi,* the pudding may be filled with date paste, walnuts, or preserved egg yolks because these items represent long life, harmony, and many children. For decoration, the top of the pudding is ornamented with pine and cypress branches, which symbolize longevity.

The distinctive qualities of glutinous rice, from which *niangao* and other New Year specialties are made, is described in a 14th-century book entitled *Essential Knowledge for Eating and Drinking* (Yinshi xuzhi). The author Jia Ming states, "its flavor is sweet; its character is warm." But, he warns, "eaten in excess it causes fevers, and it impedes the action of the pulse. Horses eating it develop stumble-feet. If young cats and dogs eat it, their legs will become bent so they cannot walk."[11] Jia Ming lived to be over one hundred years of age and attributed his longevity to the exercise of caution over what he ate and drank.

Connoisseurs of Chinese food regard the New Year cake made in Ningpo (Zhejiang Province) as the very best because it uses a glutinous rice flour made from the winter harvest. *Niangao* from Ningpo is not sweet but salty in taste, with vegetables, shredded meat, cabbage, turnip, or spinach being added to the mixture. The *niangao* from Jiangsu Province is considered noteworthy because it is made from reddish-purple rice which gives the finished cake a natural redness. The addition of pine seeds, walnuts, and sweet osmanthus, give it a distinctive flavor much appreciated in the central provinces of China.

New Year cake can be served warm or fried—every region has its preference. Some versions of this recipe use thin slices of glutinous rice cake simmered in a clear broth to which celery and shredded winter bamboo shoots are added. Epicureans consider *niangao* a wonderful main dish that is best served by itself, accompanied by a glass of fine wine.

Shepherd's Purse from the Old Village

A few days ago, my wife came back from grocery shopping in the Xidan Markets and told me that shepherd's purse was for sale there. That reminded me of the days when I lived in eastern Zhejiang. For folks there, the wild vegetable was a staple served during spring. In the villages and small townships people could pick them in their backyards. Women and children squatted on the ground, each equipped with a pair of scissors and a tiny "seed basket." The work was engaging and full of fun. In those days children used to sing:

Shepherd's purse sprayed over the head,
charming sisters are about to wed.

There have been some literary references revolving around this tiny plant. Gu Lu, writer from the Manchu dynasty, noted in his Qingjia Records: "The locals refer to the shepherd's flowers as the wild grass flowers. Since superstitions hold that on the third of March armies of ants would ascend the mountain of the stove, all the folks would place the flower around the edge of their stoves to fend off the ants. By daybreak, the streets would echo with the cries of village children selling the flowers. Because many women wear the flowers in their hairclips in the hope of improving their eyesight, the flower also came to be known also as "bright-eye flower."

But the real villagers I knew of paid no attention to this gibberish. They just mixed the flowers in their dishes, or squashed them into the glutinous rice cakes and ate them.

—Books from a Rainy Day, by Zhou Zuoren (1885–1967) (translated by the authors)

Imperial Dining

A discussion of New Year festival foods wouldn't be complete without a historical note on the elaborate dining habits of the imperial family during the Ming (1368–1644) and Qing (1644–1911) dynasties.

In the Ming courts the feast of the Great Banquet (the first of four levels of imperial banquets) was given at the New Year festival when foreign envoys were at the palace and able to attend. The rites for ceremonial visits and festive occasions were intricately complex, as one might imagine. Ranking court officials and military officers assembled outside the palace gate. Officials of the fourth rank or above were accommodated within the imperial hall. Palace guards stood on duty at the gates. Pennants were hung, the imperial dais was set in place, and service stations were arranged around the imperial dining area. As the emperor entered, wearing the royal robes and the royal crown, he received greetings from his officers and generals. The propitious phrase "may you live one thousand years"

New Year print showing preparation of an imperial banquet.

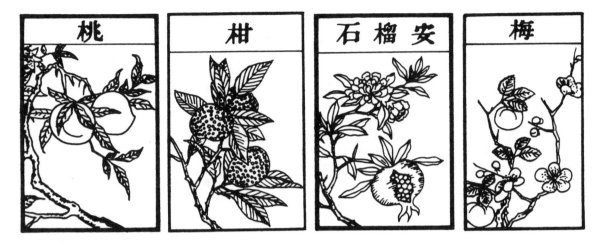

New Year fruits: peaches, orange, pomegranate, plums.

(wansui) was chorused by all attending officials. Dining commenced around midday and continued through the afternoon.[12]

As for the imperial New Year's Eve banquet in Qing times, the ceremony was as elaborate as it was in preceding dynasties. Participants took their seats inside the Forbidden Palace at the Hall of Preserving Harmony. Ninety tables, seating two each, were set with wine and dishes of food. After the emperor entered, all present took their seats. During the banquet, music played—there were Tibetan songs, Mongolian instrumentals, and Manchurian melodies, reflecting the foreign origins of the Qing dynasty emperors and many of the high officials. Clown performances, acrobatics, and lion dances were all part of the entertainment. Finally, after the food was served, the music performed and the guests had prostrated themselves for the last time in front of the emperor, the feasting ended. Officials formed ranks and filed out and the attendants were then allowed to take away the remaining sweets and fruits, known as "snatching the banquet delicacies" *(qianyen)*.[13]

Flowers

Chinese plants have always played an important role in Chinese culture. Poetry and prose abound with the symbolic and expressive allusions to flowers. During the New Year, in the south of China, plants and flowers can be seen everywhere. Flower markets are filled with blossoms just opening, which signify the fresh and invigorating hopes for a prosperous New Year. A few favorite plants traditionally used to ornament one's home during the New Year are:

Narcissus *(shuixian)*—good fortune and prosperity
Camellia *(chahua)*—springtime
Evergreen *(wannianqing)*—ten thousand years
Peach *(taozi)*—longevity
Buddha hand citron *(foshou)*—happiness and longevity
Quince *(tiegeng haitang)*—flower for the Chinese New Year in San Francisco

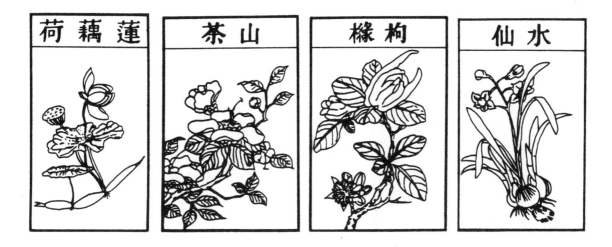

New Year flowers: lotus, camellia, hand citron, and narcissus.

DIVINATION AND ENTERTAINMENT

Part of the Chinese New Year is a very private event that focuses exclusively on family and home. Another part, however, is very public, with noisy celebrations, entertainment on the streets, and fortunetelling at the temple.

Following the first day of the New Year, after the family has gathered around at midnight on New Year's Eve to individually wish each other good fortune and happy times ahead, a variety of shared events occur over the next two weeks: the celebration for "The Beginning of Spring" *(li-chun)* takes place; people consult the almanac and Chinese zodiac; and everyone participates in the many aspects of the Lantern Festival, from eating *yuanxiao* dumplings to chasing after the dragon-lantern procession that marks the close of the New Year celebrations. For better or worse, another year has begun.

Determining the Fortune of the Year

Having one's fortune told at the temple (Taiwan).

Telling fortunes at the neighborhood temple is a popular practice at the onset of the New Year. Usually fortunetellers will set up their stations in front of the temple. By referring to the "Eight Characters" *(bazi)* (combinations of the Heavenly Stems and Earthly Branches that symbolize the hour, day, month, and year of birth—see Chinese Calendar in the Appendix), the fortuneteller describes what one can expect from future professional relations and predicts one's personal fortune by using divination charts based on constellation signs, plants, seasons, or even the spiritual weight of one's bones.

With knowledge of the Eight Characters, and particularly of the zodiac sign governing one's birth, the fortuneteller can delve more deeply to determine how "the animal that hides in your heart will affect your destiny."

Zodiac Animals

In Chinese fortunetelling, the 12 zodiac animals are used to label each year in a sequence of 12 years, and the characteristics and promise of success associated with each sign make consulting one's animal forecast an enjoyable pastime of the New Year.

According to the rules of astrology, the 12 animals correspond to the 12 Earthly Branches. Five cycles of 12 years each make up one complete cycle of 60 years. The 60-year, or sexagenary cycle, forms the basis of the Chinese calendar. Turning 60 years of age is a cause for a major birthday celebration because the celebrant has thus completed one full cycle.

During the 60-year cycle each animal sign or Earthly Branch is combined with the Five Elements (wood, fire, metal, water, and earth) and each Heavenly Stem is associated with the Five Colors (azure, red, yellow, white, and black). The Five Elements are further split into magnetic poles called the *yin* (associated with negative forces) and the *yang* (associated with the positive). Thus, 1992 in astrological terms is the Year of the (positive) Water Monkey, or in terms of its color-animal combination, the Year of the Black Monkey.

A festival participant as the God of Longevity during a San Francisco Chinese New Year parade.

The cycle for recording years starts with the rat and follows with the ox, tiger, rabbit, dragon, snake, horse, ram, monkey, rooster, dog, and pig.

The significance of their sequence and how these 12 animals were chosen is the source, as one might expect, of many legends. One legend maintains that Buddha invited all animals to a gathering before he departed from earth, but that these 12 creatures were the only ones who appeared. As a token of his gratitude, he named a year after each animal in the order of their arrival.

Another legend attributes the choice and sequence to the order in which the animals of the world answered a banquet invitation delivered by the Jade Emperor. Still another story orders the animals according to how they finished in a contest where they were asked to cross a large river. The rat, who rode the ox's back, jumped off at just the right moment and won the race; the ox came in second, and the boar, who was slothful and lazy, finished last.

Processions of the zodiac animals have been a part of New Year festivities as far back as some 1,500 years when the costumed participants,

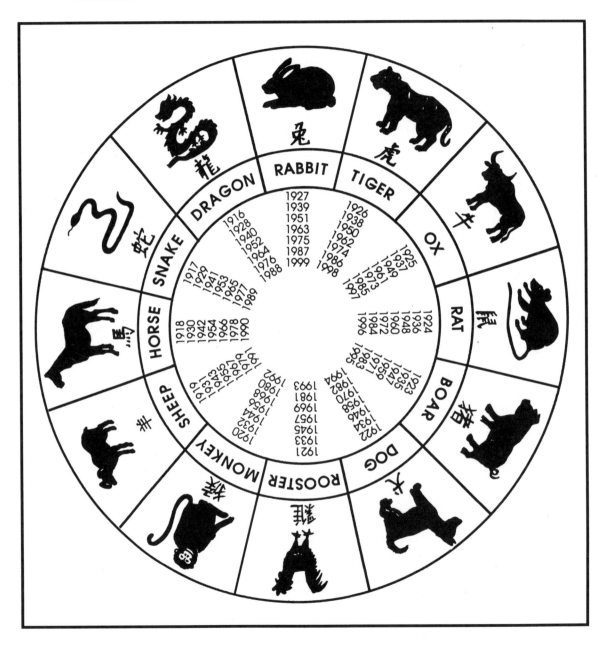

led by a sorcerer, paraded through the town to expel evil spirits. Over the ages, such ancient rites of exorcism have given way to charming zodiac customs. For example, in North China, children up to the age of 15 carry candles in the shape of their birth animal during the Lantern Festival. They try to guess who is older or younger based on the participants' animal signs.

Lunar Zodiac Chart

(Birth dates should be checked against a more detailed lunar calendar because years overlap the Gregorian calendar. For example, a person born in 1955 can be either a Horse or a Ram, because the the period of February 3, 1954 to January 23, 1955 was the Year of the Horse on the lunar calendar, and the Year of the Ram began on January 24, 1955.)

The basic personality characteristics associated with each creature are as follows:

Rat —*thrifty, quick-tempered and charming*

Ox —*stubborn, patient, trusting, dependable*

Tiger —*sensitive, passionate and daring*

Rabbit —*affectionate and cautious, good head for business*

Dragon —*full of vitality and strength, sets high standards*

Snake —*deep thinker and soft-spoken*

Horse —*cheerful, perceptive and quick-witted, loves to be where theaction is*

Ram —*strong beliefs, compassionate, accomplished in the arts*

Monkey —*inventor and improviser*

Rooster —*sharp and neat, extravagant in dress, prefers working alone*

Dog —*loyal, trustworthy and faithful, makes a good but somewhat reluctant leader*

Pig —*studious, well-informed, reliable*

How the Eight Characters Can Divine One's Future

How the Eight Characters can divine one's future is described in the Ming dynasty novel, *The Golden Lotus*. Here, an immortal prophesies about the future of Hsi-men Ch'ing (Ximen Ching):

"Sir," the Immortal said, "tell me first the eight words of moment in your honourable life, and I will relate the future for you." Hsi-men Ch'ing told him the Eight Characters, saying that his animal was the Tiger, his age twenty-nine, and the hour of his birth, noon on the twenty-eighth day of the seventh month. The Immortal silently made some calculations upon his fingers and said: "Sir, your horoscope would appear to show the year as *Wu Yin,* the month as *Hsin Yu (xin you),* the day as *Jen Wu (ren wu)* and the hour as *Ping Wu (bing wu)* . . . Your Eight Characters are certainly clear and unusual. But though this is so, you are adversely affected by the Eighth Element in *Wu,* seeing that you were born between the seventh and eighth months, a fact which gives you too great physical vigour. Fortunately the day of your birth was *Jen Wu* and the Water Element of *Kuei (gui)* comes between *Tzu (zi)* and *Ch'ou (chou),* thus producing an equilibrium between water and fire, and putting beyond doubt the fact that you will profit by your abilities. The hour was *Ping Wu,* and this fits in very well with *Hsin,* so you may look forward to a career of great dignity: you will prosper, be happy, and at peace all your life. Your fortune will increase; you will obtain promotion, and you are destined to leave behind you an honourable descendent. Throughout your life you will be honest and fair-dealing; when once you have made up your mind you will not change it. In joy you will be as agreeable as the breeze in spring, and in anger as terrible as the sudden thunder and fierce lightning. You will enjoy many women, great wealth, and not a few of the insignia of office, and when at last you leave this world there will be two sons to speed you on your way . . . "

—THE GOLDEN LOTUS (translated by Clement Egerton)

"Beginning of Spring"

The farmer's agricultural year was traditionally inaugurated during the "Spring Begins" *(lichun),* the first of the 24 "solar breaths" or "joints" (periods of 15 days each, calculated according to the solar rather than the lunar calendar and named after the characteristics of each season (see Appendix for the Chinese calendar).

In old China the reception of spring was a state ceremony featuring a paper (or clay) model of a Spring Ox and a representation of its driver, Mang Shen, the patron spirit of springtime. The following is a description of the outdoor activity called the "Beating of the Spring" *(da-chun)* that took place in the 1920s:

> Arrived at an open space to the east of the city, the local magistrate, his underlings and, sometimes, the bystanders also, went through the form of beating and prodding ox and driver by way of making them work as an example to the farmers. This had to be done with bamboos decorated with strips of coloured paper at the "exact hour when spring begins." Meanwhile, in front of their houses, people stuck a large piece of hollow bamboo in the ground with chicken feathers in it, and this they still do, for we have ourselves seen it in Peking. As the feathers fly upward on the first breeze, supposed to blow at the moment when the ox is beaten, everyone knows spring has actually come.
>
> After these ceremonies, the effigies are burned, while the crowd rushes forward to catch pieces of the coloured paper as a luck-charm, and the officials go home, take off their winter fur-lined robes, and put on their spring costumes."
>
> —THE MOON YEAR, by Juliet Bredon and Igor Mitrophanow

The crowds of people who watched the procession could tell by the colors, size, and accessories of the ox and herdboy what to expect in weather for the coming year. The images were highly symbolic, being carefully prepared according to the instructions written in the first page of the Chinese almanac or *Tong shu* (The Book of Myriad Things). This book, whose core is the Chinese calendar, has been published since the ninth century and has a large circulation even today, as can be seen in Chinese bookstores and street corner magazine stands in Hong Kong, Taiwan, and San Francisco.

If one missed the procession, the first illustrated page of the almanac could tell the reader exactly what the agricultural prospects were for the coming year. One only had to be aware of the clues. For instance, if Mang Shan is wearing a hat, the year will be sunny and dry. If his hat is off, it will be cool and rainy. Shoes indicate plenty of rain, bare feet indicate a drought.

The almanac's written instructions for the ox's color are determined by the cyclical characters (10 Heavenly Stems and 12 Earthly

Branches) associated with various parts of the animal's anatomy. For example, the head of the ox corresponds to the first cyclical character associated with the year. In the case of 1990, Year of the Horse, the cyclical characters for the year are *geng wu*. Because *geng* belongs to metal and metal corresponds to white, the head of the ox in 1990 was white. The color of the body depends on the second cyclical character, in this case *wu* (horse), which corresponds to red.

Once the color is established, the prognostication for the year's weather and overall conditions can be made. Accordingly, if the head of the ox is white, there will be high winds and storms; if it is red, there will be a drought; if it is black, there will be rain; if it is yellow, there will be a heat wave; if it is green, there will be sickness.

Relationships of the Five Elements

Element	Heavenly Stem	Color	Direction
wood	*jia* and *yi*	azure	east
fire	*bing* and *ding*	red	south
earth	*wu* and *ji*	yellow	center
metal	*geng* and *xin*	white	west
water	*ren* and *gui*	black	north

The Spring Ox from the Almanac.

Building a Spring Ox
(Geng wu, 1990—Year of the Horse)

The Spring Ox is four feet high (to represent the four seasons) and eight feet long, of clay or papier mâché. The tail is 12 inches long (to represent the 12 months of the year). The color of the head, horns, ears and tail are white; the lower leg, black; belly, yellow; body, red; hooves, yellow. The tail is facing left (indicating the year belongs to the male principle, *yang*). The mouth is open (also indicating the year is *yang*). A red ramie cord tied through the cow's nose is made of mulberry wood.

Mang Shan stands three feet six-and-a-half inches high (representing 365 days of the year). He is wearing a yellow coat with a green sash. His hair is combed in two bunches on top of his head. He covers his ear with his right hand (meaning thunder claps will be minimal). The willow branch in his hands is 24 inches long (representing the 24 divisions of the year). He is standing behind the ox (because the inauguration of spring took place more than five days after the New Year), on the left-hand side (since Mang Shen is standing behind the ox, the planting will occur late in the New Year).

The Lantern Festival

The climactic night of the New Year holiday is the Lantern Festival *(deng jie)* or the Feast of the First Full Moon *(yuanxiao jie)* and is celebrated on the 15th day of the first month. The streets are filled with spectators viewing hundreds of lanterns and following gay processions of clowns, stilt walkers, lion dancers, and actors in festive costumes and painted faces.

The origin of this holiday is unclear, but it seems that at its inception, over a thousand years ago, the Lantern Festival focused on fertility. In ancient times, devotional ceremonies were conducted to usher in light and warmth after the cold of winter and to pray for plentiful spring rains.

Popular tradition for the most part ignores the ritual content of the festival and concentrates instead on stories and legends about patriotism. A tale widely circulated in a Zhejiang village tells about the defeat of the ruling Mongols, regarded as foreign invaders by the indigenous Han nationality, on the

Lantern Festival
(contemporary Chinese folk painting).

15th day of the first month. Another folktale describes the ruin of the despised Lu clan by Emperor Wen of the Han dynasty—an event that also occurred on the 15th day of the first month. According to the story, every year thereafter on the 15th, the emperor would leave his palace in ordinary dress and parade with a host of courtiers on the streets to celebrate the occasion.

The display of elaborate lanterns was a main attraction of the festival. As early as the sixth century A.D., public viewing of fancy lanterns had become a common practice. Historical accounts tell of the emperor's eloquent praise for colorfully decorated oil and lacquer lanterns. By the Tang dynasty (618–906) the Lantern Festival had become a three-day holiday, and nighttime curfews were lifted so that commoners and nobility alike could enjoy the ceremonies. In the Song dynasty (960–1279) the festival became more elaborate, the lanterns were becoming more spectacular, and the event was extended from three to five nights. When there was imperial approval of the festival, the processions and displays served to validate the prosperity of the realm and confirm the people's joy over a peaceful and prosperous reign.[14] [See color plate 2b.]

The brilliant display and wide variety of lanterns retained its popularity through the Ming and Qing dynasties and continues to be a highlight of the New Year festivities to this day. The dazzling variety of lanterns in the streets of Beijing in 1927 must have been a sight to behold:

> The varieties displayed are infinite—all shapes, materials, decorations, sizes and prices, and all alight in the open shops. Wall-lanterns to put on either side of the front door are offered in pairs. Others are sold in sets, eight or sixteen, intended to be hung together and thus form a complete picture. "Guest-lanterns"—large white silk moons decorated with the purchaser's name and lucky bats—intended to light visitors across a courtyard to the reception hall, stand ready on bamboo tripods. Cheap paper lanterns cunningly made to copy living creatures hang from the ceiling; fantastic crabs with moving claws, dragon-flies with flapping wings, birds with swaying necks. Glass or gauze panels painted with historic scenes, mounted in carved wood frames, are displayed in great variety. Inside the shops there are many special lanterns for special purposes. Of such are those in the shape of little boys, intended for presents to childless families; "heavenly lanterns" to be hoisted on a high pole in

the courtyard and decorated with fir branches; round toy-lanterns made to roll on the ground like a fire-ball; lanterns set on wheels; red paper lamps pricked with tiny pin-holes to form a lucky character, like "happiness" or "prosperity"; *"tsomateng" (zouma-deng)* or horse-racing lanterns which consist of two or more wire frames, one within the other, "arranged on the principle of the smoke-jack so that a current of air sets them revolving"; and, finally, crossword puzzle lanterns with riddles pasted on their sides intended to hang outside a scholar's home for the amusement of his literary friends.

—The Moon Year, by Juliet Bredon and Igor Mitrophanow

Nowadays, candlelit lanterns are often replaced by wall lamps, but a blending of old and new traditions still exists. In the industrial city of Harbin in northeast China, fantastic lanterns continue to be carved from large blocks of river ice—beautifully illuminated with colored electric lights and left standing, as they have for centuries, until the ice melts away with the arrival of warmer weather in the spring.

Food

During the Lantern Festival every household consumes sweet-tasting glutinous rice flour balls called *yuanxiao*. They are often eaten in a light soup named *tangyuan*. *Yuanxiao* are symbolic of the first full moon of the year and family reunion because of their perfectly round shape. *Yuanxiao* have many fillings—pastes of hawthorne, black bean, date, dark and white sesame or sweet osmanthus. In the South, pork, chicken, and vegetable fillings are popular. Although there are regional differences in taste, there is only one way to cook dumplings, which is to heat them just long enough so that the outer skin has a delicate and slippery consistency.

In the North, custom requires that *yuanxiao* be made on the seventh day of the New Year and sold on the eighth. One can buy these treats in restaurants throughout the Lantern Festival until the 18th of the first month. After that date, the dumplings are no longer available.

Other versions of *yuanxiao* include Mongolian butter dumplings, which are mildly sweet with a creamy aftertaste. In Tianjin the fillings are made with a mixture of honey and white grapes. Shanghai dumplings excel in both salty and sweet categories, and Zhejiang is noted for its crabmeat dumplings.

Yangge

Aside from viewing festive lanterns and snacking on rice-flour dumplings, there are many types of dances, songs, variety acts and short plays to enjoy which are particularly popular during the Lantern Festival.

Especially popular are the folksong and dance productions performed by amateur actors and musicians often called "rice-sprout songs" *(yangge)*. This particular name suggests that this tradition originated with farmers, both men and women, who sang songs as they transplanted young rice shoots in the fields. From such melodies, different localities in the North and South produced a variety of music and dance forms including

Local opera troupe performance (contemporary Chinese folk painting).

lion, dragon and donkey dances, stilt performances, juggling, pole climbing, umbrella processions and "one-female, one-clown" skits. In some areas drama was emphasized, in other places dance was highlighted. [See color plate 3a.]

But the name varies from region to region, leading some scholars to suggest that *yangge* began as a religious ritual whose origins can be traced back to the Great Exorcism, or *No* Festival.

The Great Exorcism or *No* Festival of Han times probably developed from rituals of expulsion and placation common to popular religions of many cultures. In China, the first ritual gesture is designed to rid the countryside of marauding ghosts and evil demons through martial performances such as the lion dance. Then, through folkplays and songs, one placates the inhabitants of the sacred world, receiving from the souls of ancestors and spirits of gods blessings for the new year.

The invigorating performances of dynamic and lusty *yangge* song and dance acts, along with other spirited New Year theatricals, and such practices as saying only auspicious things, were directed to this invisible audience of the dead to show them fertility, fortune, and reproductive energy, and by this means receive their assistance to ensure prosperous times ahead. The ritual mystery and spiritual vitality of *yangge* is still retained in some areas of China, but in most places the "sacred" aspects have disappeared, having gradually evolved over the centuries into popular secular entertainment.[15]

By the time of the Southern Song dynasty (1127–1279) there were a large number of amateur dance and entertainment troupes, and each village and city guild had its own dance group for festival occasions. This type of "village music" from Southern Song Lantern Festivals set the precedent for the stylistic development of *yangge* in the Qing dynasty. In addition to music and dance, Song dynasty dance troupes also staged a variety of street fare acts, with storytellers, wrestling contests, acrobatics, shadow theater, puppet shows, poetic music dramas and comic acts.

Dry Boat Plays

One of the special features of these variety shows, and still popular today, is the "dry boat" *(hanchuan)* play. Traditionally, village boys dressed up as girls and sat alluringly in a boat that never touched water. An accompanying boatman holding a bamboo pole pushed his passengers around an imaginary lake. Such scenes were meant to be imitations of romantic boating outings where the couple spent a leisurely after-noon in a boat picking lotuses. The boat is actu-ally a cloth construction that covers the performer's legs and feet to make it look as if he is sitting in it. To make the illusion more lifelike, an extra pair of "dummy" legs is visible on top of the boat.

The dry boat performance (Beijing).

     To represent the boat crossing the water, the performer uses a series of smooth dance steps; to show rocking, he faces the rower and trades off rising and falling movements. While engaged in "rowing," the boatman and seductive "girl" exchange a medley of charming folk songs.

Lion Dance

There is still more to see, especially in the realm of dance. The most widespread of all dances is the lion dance and dragon-lantern dance. At festivals, men in gigantic, colorful, papier-mâché lion heads and bodies clear the pathway for parades. Two performers skilled in this special art perform the dance—one man handles the papier-mâché head decorated with tinkling bells, painted eyes, movable jaws and lolling tongue, and another manipulates the hindquarters, all to the accompaniment of drums and gongs. The lion is in constant motion, crouching down and leaping up, bowing low and hunching his back. In some parts of China the lions are in pursuit of a ball or "pearl." In other parts, performances focus on "lion tamers" teasing the lions, or a single lion frolicking with its cubs.

Probably because the lion is not indigenous to China, the King of Beasts took on a mythical aura and a stylized form of representation many centuries ago when the lion dance originated in China. At least as early as the Eastern Han dynasty (25–220), embassies from the kingdom of Arsaces (ancient Persia) brought lions to the court as tribute. These rare and powerful animals were highly valued and symbolically associated with purity and protection. East-West contacts at this time also brought acrobats, jugglers, musicians, and conjurers into China who dramatically influenced palace entertainment.

With choreographic innovations incorporated into the dance during the Tang dynasty, this performance became increasingly vivid and expressive. Especially popular was the "Lion Dance of the Five Directions" featuring five lions costumed in different colors and standing over three yards tall. Their heads were wooden, their tails were of silk, their eyes were gilded, and their teeth were plated with silver. Twelve "lion lads" carrying red whisks teased the lions, providing an amusing and lively form of entertainment.

Nowadays the lion dance is still performed at auspicious occasions such as weddings and store openings, and is often promoted as a fundraising event for various charities. During the New Year, lucky lions are visible everywhere, prancing along shop-lined streets, promising good luck to merchants in exchange for red *hongbao* packets filled with money.

The Dragon Parade

Unlike the lion, the dragon appears far less frequently, saving his awesome image for one appearance only, which usually occurs on the last day of the Lantern Festival. Dozens of people are needed to carry the imposing wily serpent that stretches for at least 20 or 30 feet. It is constructed of bamboo rods and satiny cloth in sections of three or four feet and was traditionally illuminated by candles. Each "limb" is on a pole carried by one person who, together with the other participants, manipulates the dragon, making it sweep and wind gracefully though the streets.

The dragon is a mythical creature symbolic of vigor, fertility and spring rain, and was also an imperial emblem from the Han dynasty onward. It is a composite creature described as having the head of a camel, horns of a deer, eyes of a rabbit, ears of a cow, neck of a serpent, belly of a frog, scales of a carp, and talons of a hawk—it seems to express the life force by being a powerful summation of all these animals.

In San Francisco, the dragon, all 160 feet of him, is the highlight of the annual Golden Dragon Parade. He follows a globular ornament representing the sun, the source of his power. Accompanying the dragon is a procession of carnival-like characters. There are the Eight Immortals and the popular foursome of Monkey, Pigsy, Tripitaka, and Sandy from the novel *Journey to the West*. There's also the Big-Headed Monk dallying with the flirtatious Liu Cui, characters mentioned as early as the Yuan dynasty and later in Ming "poetic dramas." [See color plate 1a,b.]

In addition, there are more than 50 floats, marching bands, dance troupes and bell-and-drum corps featured in the parade, making it the largest event of its kind in the world. Mixing Chinese and U.S. parade themes and credits, there are floats featuring deities and creatures such as the God of Wealth (sponsored by the California Lottery) and racing horses belonging to the legendary Generals of the Five Directions (sponsored by the Golden Gate Fields and Bay Meadows race tracks).

The San Francisco celebration, which began in 1953 as a minor parade to complement the Miss Chinatown beauty contest, adds a new dimension to the traditional Lantern Festival. There's really nothing quite like it in China. Although the dragon dance and promenade of immortal celebrities are adopted from the Chinese festival, the parade itself is a purely Chinese-American invention. We have seen the birth of a new custom in the festival tradition, with a change in the ritual occurring just as other changes have through the millennia. In all likelihood, such a widely recognized and publicized event (more than one million television viewers and some 400,000 spectators) is here to stay. It will continue to herald the beginning of the New Year for many years to come and, through the image of the dragon, convey to the viewer the much sought-after traits of strength and courage.

"Dry Boat" performers from a northern Chinese village.

The Dragon Boat Festival
(5th day, 5th moon)

Duanwu Jie

The day of the Dragon Boat Festival is infused with the colors of the Five Elements—red, yellow, azure, white and black—and the lingering scent of incense and festival foods permeates the hot summer air. This is the day of the "double fifth" (fifth day of the fifth moon), which corresponds to the period around the summer solstice (June 21) and is the second of the three "Festivals of the Living." Prior to this midpoint of the year, nature is characterized by growth and ripening (the *yang* force), but from the summer solstice to the winter solstice, nature moves toward decline and decay (the *yin* force).

The festival which highlights this crucial point of the calendar dates back at least two thousand years and is rooted in fertility rites to ensure abundant rainfall in southern China. In agricultural China, the ceremonies occurred when the transplantation of young rice plants had been completed and torrential summer rains were about to begin.

Today, the Dragon Boat Festival is still widely celebrated, especially in Central and South China, with river parades, dragon boat races, and rice offerings of *zongzi* to China's earliest known poet, Qu Yuan.

DRAGON BOAT RACES

The day of the Dragon Boat Festival is filled with excitement as crowds eagerly anticipate the arrival of brightly painted and decorated boats for the annual dragon boat race. Boats from 10 to 15 miles around selected lake and riverside resorts enter the annual summer races that take place throughout South and Central China, Hong Kong, and Taiwan. The long, slender boats create an unforgettable spectacle, darting through the water with team participants paddling in unison, drums and gongs setting a push-pull rhythm for the rowers, and flags and banners rippling in the wind.

A bitter rivalry and long-harbored enmity built up between the boat teams of different villages adds tension to the air as people wait to witness crafty nautical maneuvers, capsizing boats, or ill-tempered fights. In fact, this athletic event is so intensely competitive that it was outlawed in China in the early 1900s because of the large number of fatal accidents and fights that occurred during the races. One commentator advised building smaller boats so the fighting strength of participating craft would be reduced, thereby putting an end to dangerous skirmishes.

The canoe-shaped wooden boats are huge, ranging anywhere in size from 40 to 100 feet in length. They resemble dragons, with a fiery open-mouthed head at the bow and a scaly tail at the stern. In northern Hunan the boats are painted in different colors and combinations of colors representing the Five Elements. The preferred wood for constructing the boats is fir, because its light weight makes the boats faster and easier to row and maneuver. [See color plate 3b.]

The boats are powered by as many as 80 rowers, depending on the length of the vessel (a boat of 110 feet has seats for 80 rowers; a boat of 40 feet for 20). According to a late Ming text on the dragon boat race in Hunan, the ideal crews consisted of strong, experienced men from local fishing villages. Aptly enough, they were nicknamed "water crows" *(shuilaoya)*.

In the Ming dynasty the bow was occupied by a headman who had to be of high social standing in the community. At the stern was an endman who steered the boat by means of a 20-foot-long oar. In the middle of the boat was a flagman who guided the boat with flag signals and a drummer and clapper who set the rhythm for the oarsmen. A sorcerer called the "old mountain master" *(shanlaoshi)* was employed to purify or "brighten" the boat by scattering buckwheat from stem to stern and lighting fire to this grain.

The boats were identified with different clans or guilds (usually six boats representing six different clans participated in the actual race). Each boat had its own guardian deity (often the spirits of drowned people), special banners, and different uniforms designed to coordinate with the color scheme painted on the dragon head, scales, and tail of each group's dragon boat.

Historically, rivals tried to outwit one another during the race by sometimes tiring out an opponent through sudden advances and stops or by secretly moving ahead, quietly rolling up the flags and resting the drums. In other cases, two boats might lock each other in an L-shaped maneuver or three boats might become engaged in their own grappling episode—the first taunts the other two into fighting and then makes its own surprise attack on them. If a boat didn't rise to the challenge of another, it was given the derogatory epithet of "coward boat" *(quechuan)*.

The sense of expectation and tension associated with the race has probably changed little over the centuries. The following description provides a modern-day account of this sporting event as seen in Yunnan Province on Lake Er Hai:

> The race was not due to start until the afternoon but all through the morning many gaily decorated boats arrived in Haidong's bay. From the cliffs I watched sailing junks, their tall rectangular sails taut with the wind as they rounded the point. Occasionally I heard snatches of song coming from men and women crews. The dragon boats were painted with dragons and flowers; there were red and gold flags fluttering from their masts, and as they came to moor they let off strings of firecrackers . . .
>
> At noon a bugle call rang out to tell the boat crews to make ready and the crowd moved down to the lakeshore. Six boats representing six lakeside villages were each manned by seventy to eighty men, with two or three men to each oar. The oars were twelve feet long with small square paddle-blades. The race course was marked by buoys and flags, starting near the village shore and running across the bay to the temple point, where the boats had to go around the last buoy and return the same way. They would run in two heats of three with a final race between the two winners.

All six boats began by rowing a lap of honour. To try to keep their strokes in time each boat had a gong tied to its mast, and a man to beat out the rowing tempo; for encouragement they also had flute musicians and firecrackers on board. The boats moved ponderously, their long oars dipping slowly and evenly into the water, and were steered by a plank of a rudder with two men at the helm. Behind the six dragonboats came a flotilla of followers, jockeying for good positions where they could drop anchor and watch the race . . . As the starting gun fired the oarsmen scrabbled frantically with their oars at the water, few keeping time with the gongbeat, tangling their oars together, and looking from a distance more like drunken galloping centipedes . . .

Each race brought enormous excitement and the oarsmen took part with such enthusiasm that several oars got broken as they smashed together in leggy tangles. The final winner was the blue-vested team from Haidong, whose relative skill gave them the well-earned prize of 200 yuan.

—A TRAVELLER IN CHINA, by Christina Dodwell

A pair of dragon boats (contemporary Chinese folk painting).

Dragon boat races have become a widely recognized international event in recent years. Hong Kong had 26 teams from as far away as Italy at their 1990 race. The San Francisco Bay Area is also conducting its own contest with 10 different crews scheduled to enter the first competition, among them a champion women's team from Vancouver, Canada.

Origins

As noted earlier, historical studies indicate that the origin of the dragon boat race is associated in some way with fertility and the growth of rice in southern China. Because rice was the sustenance of the living, every means to ensure a good harvest was practiced. This entailed special rites and ceremonies in honor of the Dragon God, who controlled the rivers and rainfall. In ancient China, tribespeople from the South actually worshiped the dragon as their totem, tattooing their bodies with dragons and shaving their heads. They considered themselves descendents of the dragon and celebrated *Duanwu Jie* as a festival day of the dragons. Dragon boat races may have been held either to please these aquatic creatures or as a type of sympathetic magic that induced the dragons of the air to imitate the terrestrial battle, which is one way to secure rain.

Another explanation for the festival links the delicate process of transplanting rice with the ritual simulation of ancestral visits through the annual dragon boat race. The boat crews, representing their dead forbears, ride dragon boats (which are symbolically related to all-powerful water dragons) in the direction of the fields where the rice has just been transplanted. During the "ancestors' visit" to the land of the living, they restore the power of the rice seedlings—which had been moved from small beds and "drowned" in larger, flooded fields. The transplanted rice is considered to be in the same state as a drowned person, so the "ancestors," while rowing the dragon boats, recall its soul *(hun)* through songs and drumming. As for the racing of dragon boats, this contest, in effect, represents one clan's struggle against the ancestors of alien lineages whose negative influences might impede the growth of rice. The Dragon Boat Festival ends with the triumphant ancestors taking away all the bad tidings as they return to the land of the dead. As a final tribute, departing offerings of food are made to them for their long passage home.[1]

The dramatic ritual may have even more primal roots than this. It has been suggested that the earliest dragon boat contests were violent struggles where at least one boat had to capsize and one person had to drown as an offering to the river gods. The fertility of the fields was secured—through human sacrifice. In parts of South China, early Tai tribespeople acquired human sacrifices by head-hunting, believing that the gods required vigorous offerings of human life to ensure bountiful harvests. Later, these ceremonies gave way to swimming and wading contests where at least one participant inevitably drowned. Eventually, boat races were substituted for swimming contests in Central and South China with unavoidable "accidents" and drownings considered a sort of predetermined sacrifice for the river gods.[2]

Qu Yuan

If one were to inquire about the origin of the Dragon Boat Festival, most Chinese would claim that it was to recall the soul of Qu Yuan, a poet who served as a loyal minister in the third century B.C. He tried to advise the king on how to keep peace with neighboring states, but his advice was rejected and he was banished from the kingdom. When he later learned that the capital city was destroyed in war, he despaired and wrote one of China's most famous elegies, the *Li sao,* (Lament on Encountering Sorrow). Then he threw himself into the Milo River (in Hunan Province) and drowned.

The people got into their boats and raced to find him, but to no avail. When they realized he had drowned, they threw rice into the water as a sacrifice or, according to some versions of the legend, to prevent the fish from eating his body. To this day, dragon boat races are held to commemorate the tragic event by reenacting the search for Qu Yuan.

Qu Yuan and His Lament

Ch'u Yuan [Qu Yuan], who was born on a Tiger day, was a minister of the Chou [Zhou] Kingdom. He advised the king not to go to war against Ch'in [Qin], but the king listened to the warmongers and fought a losing war. Because he had expressed an unpopular opinion, Ch'u Yuan was banished. He had to leave the Center; he roamed in the outer world for the rest of his life, 20 years. . . . His love for his country was not returned. . . . He sang poems wherever he went, haggard and poor, always homesick, roving from place to place on foot like an old beggar. . . .

He wrote a poem made of one hundred and seventy questions with no answers. "Soothsayers who use tortoise and yarrow," he asked, "what is the order of creation?" "Who built the sky?" "Where does it end?" "Why do I try to bank up the waters in the dark sea when I am not a great whale?"

From his dragon boat, he looked down at his home and realized that escape and return were equally impossible.

At last he walked along the Tsanglang River while reciting poems. He met a fisherman and told his story again. He had seen the entire corrupt world, and "the crowd is dirty."

"Why should you be aloof?" asked the fisherman. "When the water is clear, I wash my tassels, but when it too muddy for silk, I can still wash my feet."

Upon hearing these words, Ch'u Yuan decided that he would use the river too. He sang all his poems and his elegy, his requiem. He danced at the edge of the river to make his last moments happier. He threw himself into the water and drowned. "There is no wisdom in the world," says the commentary to the Li Sao. "Its people are too corrupt to deserve a man like this."

—CHINA MEN, by Maxine Hong Kingston

Zongzi

The story of Qu Yuan also gives us the origin of a tasty glutinous rice dumpling called *zongzi,* a popular street-fare specialty consumed during the Dragon Boat Festival. According to the tale, the soul of Qu Yuan appeared before a group of fishermen, crying out to them that he was starving because a dragon was eating his rice offerings.

The offerings consisted of bamboo tubes filled with glutinous rice. In order to prevent the dragon from stealing them, Qu Yuan ordered the tubes to be closed with lily leaves and tied with multi-colored threads.

Today's *zongzi* is made similarly, with a serving of rice wrapped in leaves and tied together with string. The way the string is wound and knotted tells what ingredients are inside—pickled egg, beans, dates, fruits, yam, gelatin pudding, walnuts, or melon seeds.

Preparing zongzi (contemporary Chinese folk painting).

There are many different kinds of *zongzi,* each with its own particular flavor, shape, and type of leaf for wrapping. *Zongzi* is usually four-sided with pointed or rounded ends. Sometimes it is in the shape of a cone or cylinder. The glutinous rice mixture is wrapped in leaves of wild rice, palm or bamboo. Bamboo-leaf *zongzi* is a specialty of South China.

As for flavor, the Beijing style is the sweetest, with a filling of coarse bean paste. Guangdong *zongzi* is either sweet-tasting, with a walnut, date or bean filling, or salty with fillings of ham, egg, salted meat, roast chicken, duck, chestnuts or mushrooms. In Taiwan, vegetarian *zongzi* is made with dry peanut flakes; meat-filled *zongzi* consists of fresh pork, chicken or duck with egg yolk, mushroom, dried shrimp, or fried scallions.

Talismans and Charms

The day of the Double Fifth is characterized by the struggle between the dual forces of the *yin* and *yang* as the waxing *yang* reaches a culminating point with the arrival of the summer solstice and the *yin* principle, symbolizing darkness and dampness, comes fully into play.

This is the hottest month of the year, when evil vapors abound, with the fifth day of the fifth month, in particular, being considered the most "poisonous." Every attempt is made to harmonize both the *yin* and the *yang* so that danger and disease can be avoided.

The dragon boat races were one of several ways to dispel evil. At the end of the contest, the boats' crews would cast offerings into the river so that pestilence and bad tidings would float away downstream. Dragon boat races alone, however, were not enough, and traditionally other precautions were taken.

On the front door of every household, bouquets of aromatic plants, assembled from sprigs of garlic, bunches of mugwort, and leaves of sweet-flag were tied together and displayed to ward off disease. Mugwort and sweet-flag were considered especially efficacious because the leaves of the former looked like a tiger and those of the latter were pointed like demon-killing swords. Their strong odor was believed to be an effective combatant against evil. An additional precaution required the wearing of small sachets filled with pungent herbs and spices.

Five Poisons

Perhaps the most interesting and powerful of the Double Fifth charms is the "Five Poisons" *(wudu)* motif. The animals represented are the snake, centipede, scorpion, lizard, and toad (sometimes the spider replaces one of these creatures). Their images are embroidered on clothing, stamped on cakes, and engraved on paper charms, with the idea of avoiding bites from them or, as some suggest, to counteract other kinds of poisons with the accumulated poison of the five.

Another explanation regarding their potency suggests that their collective powers are condensed into the one creature found alive if they are all put together in a single container. The surviving creature is then used to make love charms and magic potions.

The *wudu* motif is commonly seen today throughout China appliquéd onto everything from vests and aprons to backpacks and shoulder bags. The pervasiveness of the motif in contemporary times, however, has more to do with mass-marketing than any religious belief.

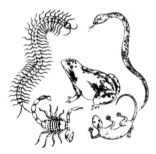

The "five poisons": centipede, snake, scorpion, toad, and lizard.

Five Colors

Another protective practice especially popular with children involves wearing five colored threads or ribbons of silk. These "threads of life" were given as gifts to families for the purpose of averting bad influences. Five colored ornaments were worn in the hair, and even *zongzi* was originally tied with five colored threads.

The five colors are a powerful motif because each color is associated with one of the Five Elements (azure=wood, red=fire, yellow=earth, white=metal, and black=water). The elements, which are five natural forces, work together in a cyclical order to represent periods of rise and decay, production and destruction. Wood prevails over earth; metal prevails over wood; fire over metal; water over fire; and earth over water. Thus, by symbolizing the essence of creation, the endless cycle of elements and their correlations with colors, directions, seasons, and so on, are especially effective in banishing pernicious influences.

Zhong Kui

Of the various images of healers and exorcists that make their annual appearance on the day of the Dragon Boat Festival, the most popular are pictures of the monster-scholar Zhong Kui gobbling up ghosts or brandishing his sword.

Zhong Kui was a tragic figure who killed himself out of shame on the steps of the imperial palace because he was unjustly defrauded of a first class rank in the civil service examinations. (Another legend claims he was denied scholastic honors because of his ugly features.) Emperor Minghuang (712–756), however, honored him with an imperial burial, and out of gratitude Zhong Kui vowed to free the world of ghosts and demons in his afterlife.

Emperor Minghuang had a nightmare in which a troublesome imp dressed in red trousers, with one shoe on and one shoe off, was cavorting in the royal chambers, playing with an embroidered box and a jade flute. The emperor was furious with the creature, who called himself "Emptiness and Ruin" ("Emptiness" because in emptiness one can move about as one desires and "Ruin" because it changes people's happiness to sorrow). Suddenly, the spirit of Zhong Kui appeared wearing the robes, hat, and black boots of a Chinese scholar and crushed the sprite with his bare hands. The emperor woke from his dream and asked the court painter Wu Daozi (b. ca. 700) to paint the demon-queller Zhong Kui. Supposedly, this portrait of the ghost-catcher with bulging eyes was so well done that it became the model for all subsequent images of Zhong Kui. [See color plate 6a.]

A fleet of dragon boats (contemporary Chinese folk painting).

1a, b. Golden Dragon Parade, Year of the Snake (San Francisco).
(Photos by Kim Raftery)

2a. Door gods on a village house (Beijing).

2b. A blue tiger lantern for the Lantern Festival.

2c. Character for "fortune"; to be hung upside down on the front door.

3a. Stilt walkers at a New Year village celebration (Beijing).

3b. Finishing a dragon boat parade on the Yangtze River.

4a. A display of dishes prepared on the 9th day of the 9th month, with entreés crafted of flour dough to resemble seafood and other delicacies.

4b. Taoist priest performing rites for the Hungry Ghost Festival (Taiwan).

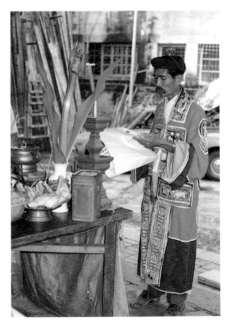

5a. A pair of ghostly
"patrolmen."
(Taiwan).

5b. Sorrowful face of
Grandfather Seven who
hung himself out of
remorse over his friend's
death (Taiwan).

6a. The demon queller Zhong Kui, portrayed in Chinese folk painting.

6b. Cowherd and Weaving Maiden portrayed in a Chinese lunar calendar (Hui County, China).

7. Young Islamic girl silently anticipates a delicious feast at the end of the Ramadan fast.
(Photo by Charlotte Temple)

8. A funeral procession (contemporary Chinese folk painting).

9a. The rats' wedding procession, furtively regarded by a crouching cat over their heads (Chinese woodblock print).

9b. Traditional version of young love: reading together under the moon (contemporary Chinese folk painting).

10a. Miao women of
Guizhou dressed in festive
costumes.
(Photo by How Man Wong)

10b. Spectacular silver
headdress and jewelry
adorning the traditional
Miao costume.

11. Young women of Dai nationality splashing water during their Sixth month festival.

12a. Jingpo tribespeople of Yunnan parade with peacock feathers.

12b. Across the wide open plains of the Sino-Soviet border, Kirghir horsemen engage in the sport of sheep tugging.

(Photos by How Man Wong)

THREE

The Mid-Autumn Festival

(15th day, 8th moon)

Zhongqiu Jie

The Mid-Autumn Festival focuses on the shining harvest moon, and because of this, is perhaps the most romantic of the three "Festivals of the Living." The celebration falls on the 15th day of the eighth lunar month, exactly in the middle of the autumn season (the autumn season being the seventh, eighth and ninth lunar months), or in the Gregorian calendar sometime around mid-September, at the time of the full moon commonly called Harvest Moon or Hunter's Moon in U.S. lore.

This is the time set aside in a busy agricultural year to enjoy the successful reaping of rice and wheat with offerings of melons, round cakes, and pomegranates presented by women in honor of the moon. At this time, the moon's orbit is at its lowest angle to the horizon, which makes it appear brighter and larger than at any other time of the year.

Originally, this was an outdoor festival. With the heavy labors of farming over, people planned a leisurely day of thanksgiving and pleasure, hiking and picnicking in the valleys and mountains. Today, it is still an occasion for outdoor reunions where friends and relatives gather together to eat "moon cakes" and watch the moon, its perfectly round shape forming the ideal symbol of familial harmony and unity.

A Child Meets the Moon Lady

In 1918, the year that I was four, the Moon festival arrived during an autumn in Wushi that was unusually hot, terribly hot. When I awoke that morning, the fifteenth day of the eighth moon, the straw mat covering my bed was already sticky. Everything in the room smelled of wet grass simmering in the heat . . .

"No time to play today," said Amah, opening the lined jacket. "Your mother has made you new tiger clothes for the Moon Festival . . ." She lifted me into the pants. "Very important day, and now you are a big girl, so you can go to the ceremony . . ."

"Who is coming today?" I asked.

"Dajya [Dajya]"—All the family—she said happily. "We are all going to Tai Lake. The family has rented a boat with a famous chef. And tonight at the ceremony you will see the Moon Lady."

"The Moon Lady! The Moon Lady!" I said, jumping up and down with great delight. And then, after I ceased to be amazed with the pleasant sound of my voice saying new words, I tugged Amah's sleeve and asked: "Who is the Moon Lady?"

"Chang-o [Chang E]. She lives on the moon and today is the only day you can see her and have a secret wish fulfilled."

"What is a secret wish?"

"It is what you want but cannot ask," said Amah.

"Why can't I ask?"

"This is because . . . because if you ask it . . . it is no longer a wish but a selfish desire," said Amah. "Haven't I taught you—that it is wrong to think of your own needs? A girl can never ask, only listen."

"Then how will the Moon Lady know my wish?"

"Ai! You ask too much already! You can ask her because she is not an ordinary person."

Satisfied at last, I immediately said: "Then I will tell her I don't want to wear these clothes anymore."

"Ah! Did I not just explain?" said Amah. "Now that you have mentioned this to me, it is not a secret wish anymore."

—THE JOY LUCK CLUB, by Amy Tan

MOON MYTHOLOGY

In Chinese mythology the moon is the dwelling place of the immortals, and all the myths associated with the moon relate to longevity. On the eve of the Moon Festival storytellers recite the tales of the Moon Palace and its inhabitants to circles of eager young listeners.

The most endearing lunar character is probably the short-tailed rabbit who pounds the elixir of immortality with a mortar and pestle underneath a grove of cassia trees. The rabbit was given the honor of adorning the moon because of his extreme reverence for Buddha. According to an old Buddhist tale, the forest animals large and small once busied themselves preparing offerings to the Buddha, who in the form of a saint had asked for food and water from his followers. Each creature scurried around to bring the best it could find or catch. The rabbit, embarrassed by his meager collection of herbs and grasses, caught sight of the cooking flames and leaped into the fire, offering the best sacrifice he could possibly provide: himself.

Next to him is the woodcutter Wu Gang, eternally sentenced by the Jade Emperor to the task of chopping down a cassia tree for transgression while studying to become an immortal. Unfortunately for Wu Gang, every time he completes an axe cut, the tree miraculously closes up again.

The most popular inhabitant of the moon is the goddess Chang E, who rules over the lunar "Palace of Great Cold." Her sad tale describes the separation from her husband Hou Yi, master archer of the skies. He was responsible for shooting down nine of the ten suns that appeared together one day and burned so brightly the very existence of all living beings on earth was threatened. As a reward for extinguishing all but one sun, he was given the elixir of life from the Queen Mother of the West.

Hou Yi stored the elixir away vowing to fast one year to show his sincerity in cultivating immortality. However, Chang E discovered the magic solution and swallowed it. Suddenly she began to rise and flew all the way to the moon where, as some legends describe, she was metamorphosed into a three-legged toad. (The frog, a creature of ponds and lakes, is controlled by the moon, which regulates the tides. Both the frog and moon are symbols associated with water.)

A short-tailed rabbit holding a branch of cinnamon gazes from the moon at the festive crowds below (contemporary Chinese folk painting).

Goddess Chang E rising up to the moon as pictured on a Beijing-style kite.

From that day on Chang E ruled over the lunar kingdom while her husband Hou Yi governed the solar realm. The two are said to meet once a month on the 15th day, when the moon is full. That is the conjunction of the *yin* and *yang* principles, when the moon, it is observed, shines most brilliantly.

The other well-known lunar deity is the matchmaker Yuexialaoye, the old man in the moon who presides over all earthly marriages. He is often depicted playing chess with the God of Longevity in a mountain cave. Whoever chances to watch the game will find that many years have passed upon returning home.

Many of the moon motifs come into play during a special mid-autumn ceremony held among the Tanka, a minority people in southern China. According to the tradition for newlyweds, a toad and hare are placed underneath a cinnamon tree located outside the bridal bedroom. The bridal bed is called the "Toad Palace." An old woman acting the role of Queen Mother of the West offers cinnamon cakes and words of marital advice. The bride and bridegroom, standing in the moonlight, are presented to their families. The ceremony concludes when they enter the bridal chamber, which is called the "Moon Palace."[1]

Offerings and Food

During the Mid-Autumn Festival altars were traditionally set up in family courtyards under the moon. The first decoration purchased for the celebration table was a clay statue of the Moon Hare or the "Gentleman Rabbit" (Tu'er Ye). In old Beijing, merchants had stalls filled with rabbit statues piled four or five levels high and located at all city gates and crossroads. The largest sculpture was over two feet tall; the smallest about an inch high. All the rabbits had long ears and a three-cornered mouth; some were dressed in robes and bonnets, others in military armor accentuated with large flags. Offerings of yellow beans and cockscomb flowers were made to the rabbit in the moon as these things were also favored by immortals.

There were also moon palace posters *(yueguang ma'er)* constructed of bamboo and paper. The upper part of the poster featured the image of a heavenly bodhisattva, and below was a picture of the jade rabbit standing under the cassia tree pounding the elixir of immortality. Three paper pennants were placed at the top of the assemblage. After the effigy was offered to the moon, children burned it. Any remaining moon poster flags were carried around by children who used them to play games of tag. According to an old folk tradition, if children were tapped on the rear end by a moon staff, they would no longer have any problems with bed wetting!

When night fell, the women of the family would prepare plates filled with round fruits, apples, pomegranates, honey peaches, crab apples, sour betel nuts, and grapes, all fragranced with the scent of rose blossom incense.

The shape of the fruits symbolizes the fullness of the moon and family harmony. In some areas pears were excluded from the traditional fruits displayed because the word for "pear" *(li)* is pronounced the same as the word for "separation" and would be considered an inauspicious offering. In addition, teacups were placed on a stone table in the garden. The family would pour tea and chat, sipping and conversing, waiting for the perfect moment—when the reflection of the full moon appeared in the center of their cups.

Imperial dishes included nine-jointed lotus roots symbolizing peace, and watermelons cut in the shape of lotus petals symbolizing reunion.

Of course, today the distinctive offering of the feast is the round, sweet-filled moon cake *(yuebing)* made of flaked pastry. Imperial chefs made them as large as several feet in diameter, carved with designs of Chang E, the moon palace, or cassia trees. Ordinary cakes, however, are only a few inches in diameter. Arrangements of moon cakes were piled high to resemble a pagoda, and usually numbered 13 per serving—13 being the number of months in a full lunar year. The fillings include melon seeds, orange peel, cassia bloom, walnut, date paste, and smashed bean. The mooncakes of Guangdong are most popular, with fillings of egg yolk, lotus seed paste, and coconut.

Autumn mooncakes were also the means, according to folk legend, for overthrowing the foreign Mongols of the Yuan dynasty (1279–1368). The time and place for the revolution against Kublai Khan's descendents were hidden inside the mooncakes which were sent to friends and relatives at festival time in the year 1353. The secretly planned midnight massacre of the Mongols led by Liu Bowen, intrepid counselor to the founding emperor of the Ming dynasty, resulted in the capture of a strategically important prefecture, which hastened the downfall of the dynasty.[2]

Would the old connoisseur have enjoyed this mooncake?

During the Qing dynasty (1644–1911) the rites of moon worship became highly elaborate. Mooncakes were renamed "moonflowers" because the word for mooncake, *yuebing,* sounded the same as the word for menstruation (literally, "monthly sickness"). The Empress Dowager Ci Xi, who was especially enamored with the festival, staged rituals for the moon lasting from the 13th through the 17th day of the eighth lunar month. The days preceding the 15th were called "Welcoming in the Holiday," the days after the 15th "The Closing of the Holiday." On these four days the empress enjoyed eating a special roast dish auspiciously called "Happiness, Prosperity, Longevity Roast." The "Happiness" portion of the dish consisted of pieces of chicken and pheasant; "Prosperity" was a mixture of rice and venison, and "Longevity" was slices of lamb.

After blessing and consuming this feast the imperial party would take a long stroll, perhaps view a new play, or listen to music and song.

Mooncakes and Tea Pastries from Old Beijing

I must admit to being somewhat prejudiced against Chinese things made in the 20th century and having an almost religious respect for traditions pertaining to matters of sensory pleasure. As I sauntered by the old buildings of Xisi, the over ten-foot-high signboard for the Chamber of Eccentric Flavors always made my heart leap in fits of secret longing. The blurred and faded calligraphy on the board not only signified that the shop had been in existence since the days before the Boxer Rebellion, but it also conveyed a vague reverie of a life that was at once gentle and gracious, where thoughts that arose in quiet contemplation ascended and floated, accompanied by the smoke from the burning incense.

I no longer burn incense these days. Despite my intense interest, I have never dared to actually venture into an incense shop, for fear of the artificial perfume they mix into their products these days and the resultant heartbreak it would give. Aside from simple daily necessities, our lives are quite colorless without some adornments in the spirit of pure frivolousness. Woe to the lives in China today, a parade through extreme dryness and barrenness. After ten years of wandering around the old capital, I never did find mooncakes and pastries as good as they used to make them.

— BOOKS FROM A RAINY DAY by Zhou Zuoren (1885–1967) (translated and excerpted by the authors)

Twilight Games

The mystique of the moon festival, its poetry and magic, was expressed in a number of traditional games or twilight dances of men, women and children on or surrounding the 15th of the eighth month. Many of the games had to do with flights of the soul, spirit possession, or fortunetelling.

These rural performances were studied by ethnographer Chao Wei-pang from research conducted in Guangdong Province in the 1920s and 1930s. He described a drama entitled "Ascent into Heaven" *(shang-tiantang)* which featured a young lady who was selected from a circle of women to "ascend" into the celestial realm. Enveloped in the fragrance of burning incense, she described the beautiful sights and sounds she encountered.

"Descent into the Garden" *(lohuayuan)* was played with a younger set of girls and described each girl's visit to the heavenly garden, which according to legend contained a flowering tree that represented her. The number and color of flowers indicated the number and sex of the children she would bear in her lifetime.

Men engaged in a pastime called "Descent of the Eight Immortals" *(jiangbaxian)*. Here, one of the Eight Immortals took possession of the player, who assumed the role of a scholar or warrior.

Children liked to play "Encircling a Toad" *(guanxiamo)*—the toad, of course, being the three-legged creature inhabiting the moon. A group of participants formed a circle around the player who was chosen to be Toad King and chanted a song that transformed the boy into a toad. He then jumped about like a real toad until water was sprinkled on his head and he stopped! As for teenagers, a Chinese-American woman tells the following story of how she celebrated the moon festival in San Francisco in the 1950s:

On the early evening of the Moon Festival, my two girlfriends and I walked up to Coit Tower to view the moon. We carried the necessary food items in brown paper sacks all the way up to the tower. On a flat area near the tower we laid out a red cloth on which we strategically placed oranges, moon cakes, spirit money in gold and silver paper, and other "goodies" that did not relate to the moon festival but gave us an excuse to enjoy American junk food.

When the moon was at its fullest, we all prayed to that moon in hopes that at some future date we would all be blessed with wonderful spouses. . . . Back home in Fresno, my parents would just settle us all out in the yard during the Moon Festival and we would nibble moon cakes, sip tea, and enjoy the moon . . . nothing fancy. In San Francisco, wealthy Chinese families reserve tables at fancy Chinese restaurants or have elaborate dinner parties for this occasion.

Moon Poetry

DRINKING ALONE BENEATH THE MOON

A pot of wine among the flowers:
I drink alone, no kith or kin near.
I raise my cup to invite the moon to join me;
It and my shadow make a party of three.
Alas, the moon is unconcerned about drinking,
And my shadow merely follows me around.
Briefly I cavort with the moon and my shadow:
Pleasure must be sought while it is spring.
I sing and the moon goes back and forth,
I dance and my shadow falls at random.
While sober we seek pleasure in fellowship;
When drunk we go each our own way.
Then let us pledge a friendship without human ties
And meet again at the far end of the Milky Way.

—Li Bo (701–762), from SUNFLOWER SPLENDOR (translated by Irving Y. Lo)

A TRAVELER'S MOON

I, a traveler, came from south of the river,
When the moon was only a crescent.
In my long, distant journeying,
I've seen thrice its clear light in full.
At dawn I travel with a waning moon;
When night falls, I lodge with the new moon.
Who says that the moon has no feeling?
It has kept me company for hundreds of miles.
In the morning I set out from the bridge of the Wei River,
In the evening I enter the streets of Ch'ang-an (Changan).
But I wonder about the moon tonight:
In whose home will it be a guest?

—Bo Juyi (772–846), from SUNFLOWER SPLENDOR (translated by Chiang Yee)

New Year print: gods of Health, Wealth and Prosperity.

FESTIVALS OF THE DEAD

ONE

Clear Brightness Festival
(April 4, 5, or 6)

Qingming Jie

A solar festival, and therefore celebrated on fixed dates, the Qingming Festival starts two weeks after the vernal equinox, when the air and light become clear and pure, the grass turns green, and flowers begin to bloom. The struggle against the chill of winter is over and people feel rejuvenated by the warmth of the sun and the energy of spring. Qingming (literally "Clear Brightness") usually corresponds to the fifth of April in the Gregorian calendar. Like the secular side of Easter, or the rites of spring in various cultures, it is a springtime ceremony, marking the onset of planting, the rebirth of nature, and the beginning of outdoor activity.

In ancient times, Qingming was a holiday celebrated by dancing, singing and picnicking. Young girls and boys would court each other, whirling together through the air on merry-go-rounds and swings. Eggs would be boiled, colored, and then broken to symbolize the opening and dispersal of all life. As part of the fertility rites, the emperor planted trees on the palace grounds—an emblem of the renewal of spring. Villagers would place pine branches symbolizing long life in front of their doors and hang sprigs of willow under the eaves of their homes as symbols of life and a talisman against the forces of darkness.

Over time, however, this unrestrained holiday of life renewal gave way to a day focusing on death, a time of quiet solitude and familial closeness to commemorate departed ancestral spirits. This shift from lively, outdoor romanticism to subdued graveside worship occurred over a period of many centuries. A festival of life, which originally had nothing to do with death, became one of the "Festivals of the Dead."

This transition begins to make sense if one understands that, according to the Chinese, the dead are intimately connected with life and the distinction between living and dead perhaps is not as sharp as in the West today. The dead are believed to be responsible for ensuring fertility in the family as well as in the fields. Sacrifices of food and spirit money are made at springtime to keep the ancestors in good humor so that the family will receive abundant blessings and good harvests, instead of sickness, misfortune and famine.

Nowadays, Qingming retains some of its primal immediacy, but for the most part it is observed with ceremonial meals at the side of the family tomb, a distant salute to the uninhibited celebrations of former times. On this occasion the family treads across the grass, cleaning and repairing hillside graves to tidy up and make beautiful again the homes of the dead.

Qingming Festival

During the festival of Qingming, rain drizzles without end,
A lone traveler on the road is overcome by grief.
He would like to know where to find a wineshop,
The herdboy points to the village ahead where the apricot tree blooms.

—Du Mu (803–852)(translated by the authors)

Worship at the Grave

On the Day of Clear Brightness everyone goes to family graves with hoes and brooms to cut down weeds and to sweep away dirt. It's not a mournful day but more like a picnic as families set out offerings of food and wine to share with their dead.

A man paying respects to the deceased at the family gravesite (Taiwan).

The offerings of food to ancestors presented in the family's ancestral hall are in the form of fully prepared meals accompanied by a plentiful supply of cooked rice. There are always an even number of dishes set out since sacrifices to ancestors correspond to the *yin* or "even" principle. (Sacrifices to gods are considered *yang* or "uneven," so the dishes are odd in number.) Bowls, plates, cups, soup spoons, and chopsticks are arranged with a selection of spices and seasonings such as vinegar, soy sauce, and chili paste. Savory dishes of chicken and liver, stir-fried eggs, rice cakes and any of the dishes an ancestor was particularly fond of are all unstintingly prepared and offered. Once the deceased extracts the essence of the meal, it is shared with family and friends.

Offerings at the graveside, as opposed to the ancestral hall, may, however, be far less palatable, consisting mostly of dried mushrooms, beancurd and noodles, and cured meats along with steamed buns and cakes. Some worshipers claim that the reason dry food is presented at the grave is that it is too far away to transport regular food (any cooked dishes would spoil) and dry goods are much lighter to carry. But this lack of culinary effort might also have to do with fear of the ancestor's corpse and the presence of unknown ghosts that can frequently haunt the graveside.

Food offering in front of a tombstone (Taiwan).

One's relationship with gods, ghosts and ancestors can, in fact, be symbolized through the type of ritual foods offered, which range from the raw and uncooked to the seasoned and well-simmered. Following anthropologist Emily Ahern's exploration of Chinese ancestor worship, the all-powerful gods (who occupy a level very distant from human beings) are presented with live fish, whole pigs and raw fowl—food that is for the most part untransformed. Ancestors, on the other hand, are very close to the living in the hierarchy of the spirit world. Because their souls reside in tablets displayed in the ancestral hall within the home and are considered to be trusting and accessible, food offered to them is exactly like the food of the living.

But spirits in the area around the grave, the resting place of the corpse, are somehow less predictable, and since the grave is erected outside the boundaries of the home, it can be frequented by flocks of uninvited ghosts. Thus, the food is only partially processed and far less appetizing, to mark the distance in the relationship between the living and the spirits of the tomb.

A Place for the Dead

Ancient burial mound of the First Emperor of Qin (221–206 B.C.) at Xian, Shaanxi Province.

The whole process of worship at the grave begins as soon as the coffin is placed in a trench and carefully positioned by a geomancer. It is then covered with a mound of earth. The practice of building burial mounds began during the Warring States period, around the fifth century B.C. One of the most elaborate examples of an early tomb mound is the burial site of the Emperor of Qin (221–206 B.C.), immortalized in history books as the first unifier of China. Representing the celestial order of heaven and earth, the mound was built as a four-sided pyramid of concentric tiers, towering over 120 feet high.

The common person's grave mound is less than a molehill in comparison, but large enough at least to accommodate the ranking members of the family—in other words those who have contributed most to the continuance of the family line. Thus, married couples who have children rest in the main area of the grave, while those who died unmarried or in childhood are buried near the outer boundaries of the gravesite.

Grave with ritual paper roofing at a cemetery near Taipei.

Elders of the family make at least one annual visit to the tomb in the spring during the Qingming festival. It is important to visit tombs and tend to their upkeep to show that the family has not died out. As a rule, each family traditionally had a private burial ground in the midst of fields or on a nearby hillside. Today, in many places in contemporary China, private gravesites have given way to public graveyards since available land is very scarce, and of necessity used almost solely for agricultural or industrial production to sustain China's huge population.

How to Keep the Ancestors Happy

Geomancy or *fengshui* (literally "wind-water") is the practice of divining the land according to natural phenomena, such as wind and water. How "comfortable" a grave is depends on whether the surrounding landscape is auspicious. Desirable attributes for a gravesite include a southern exposure, streams and rivers nearby, and groves of trees, preferably cypresses and pines. The geomancer, a sort of landscape architect who selects the location of sites by analyzing how they fit in with existing elements of nature, must determine whether the shape and height of the hills surrounding the grave will ensure the proper concentration of cosmic energy.

Fengshui is especially important for the site of burials, in particular the reburial, a practice of southern and southeastern China. Six or seven years after the initial burial, the corpse is disinterred, any remaining flesh is removed, the bones are rubbed clean and arranged in a ceramic urn. The urn can be placed in the original hole left by the coffin, and the site may be improved by building an elaborate stone or concrete shelter. The bones may be moved to a new location if a more comfortable site for the ancestor is desired. If a good location for final interment is found, the descendents of the deceased will be favored with health, wealth and prosperity. It is generally believed that benefits will start flowing from the grave upon the proper burial and placement of bones, but in other cases benefits can begin as soon as the first burial, if the ancestor is comfortable enough.

One of the best examples of *fengshui* can be seen in the site chosen for the imperial Ming tombs, a place of incomparable beauty located on the outskirts of Beijing. The Tianshoushan hills behind the tombs act as a natural barricade against any harmful forces blown in by the wind *(feng)* and the favorable topology allows streams *(shui)* to run in front of the tombs, thus ensuring that only amicable spirits reside in the area.

The practice of *fengshui,* although officially condemned by the government of the People's Republic of China as "superstition," is widely adopted by architects, businessmen, and the general public in Hong Kong, Taiwan, and Singapore. It's not uncommon to make a *fengshui* reading of the architectural plans any time a building is erected in these places. Unfortunately, the blueprints for Beijing's new 70-story Bank of China building in Hong Kong, designed by famed Chinese-American architect I. M. Pei, was not approved by *fengshui* masters. Its triangular construction with pointy edges, argued the geomancers, might slice through the cosmic balance of *yin-yang* forces and nick unheeding spirits. In another case, to ease the minds of the staff and patrons of Hong Kong's posh Regent Hotel, a large picture window was set up facing the Hong Kong harbor so that the nine dragons situated nearby could easily pass through the glass to the bay—an impossible task if doors or walls were placed there instead.

Geomancer's Compass

Invented more than two thousand years ago, the art of *fengshui* rests on the skilled geomancer's use of the compass. The innermost ring of the compass is marked with five directions (north, east, west, and south, plus the center) and intermediate points, such as northeast, southwest, etc., which together are associated with the Eight Trigrams (patterns of broken and unbroken lines representing the cosmos). Other categories arranged in concentric circles around the compass include the five colors, elements of nature, combinations of the Earthly Branches and Heavenly Stems, and the location of auspicious and inauspicious spirits. Family positions such as mother and father are also noted on the compass.

The geomancer consults the compass to make correlations between the directions, elements, and the shape of the surrounding landscape. For instance, the shape of the hills should be like the animal associated with that direction, *e.g.,* a bird to the south, a tiger to the west; and the features of the terrain should symbolize each of the five elements. If the shapes and configurations are perfect, all descendents of the family will prosper.[1]

Cold Food Festival

The day before the festivities of Qingming, people in certain areas of premodern China (particularly Shanxi Province), celebrated the Cold Food Festival. All fires in the kitchen were extinguished for 24 hours. Food was prepared a day before and eaten cold, and as early as the sixth century celebrants consumed a special congee called *lilao,* which was made with apricot pits and sweetened with malt sugar. Nothing hot was eaten until after Qingming day, when the fire was relit by rubbing two willow sticks together—the willow being an emblem of spring and a talisman against evil.

The background of the Cold Food Festival is linked to ancient tribal practices of sun worship and purification. The practical origins of this festival can be traced to the conqueror-nomads of the Zhou dynasty, who divided their year into sedentary winter months on the plains and active months of spring planting on fertile mountain slopes. Each year, with the onset of spring and migration to the mountains, fires had to be started anew to burn and clear the fields.[2] This transition became ceremonialized into annual rites of renewal with the Cold Food Festival representing the interruption of fire, marking the time between extinction of the old fire and the igniting of the new.

Cosmologically speaking, this festival is a symbolic celebration of the sun's victory over darkness in the spring. Fires obviously mimic the powerful source of light and warmth in the sky and are also considered purificatory in that they burn up all baneful influences in the surrounding environment.

Geomancer's compass.

The Faithful Patriot Jie Zitui

Popular tradition claims the ceremony of eating cold food originated in honor of Jie Zitui, a loyal hero who lived in the sixth century B.C. and who belongs to the same class of exiled patriots as Qu Yuan (see *Dragon Boat Festival*).

The legend surrounding Jie Zitui begins with the flight of Jie's ruler, who lived in exile with a small band of faithful followers. Jie was so devoted to the wrongly ousted marquis that he even fed him flesh from his own leg when his master was on the verge of starvation. Eventually, the marquis regained his status as a ruler and rewarded those who remained loyal to him. But Jie would take no emolument for his service, being too proud to sacrifice his integrity for material riches since he felt Heaven alone restored the marquis to his rightful position. Jie then returned to the mountains to live as a hermit, refusing to return to assume any civic responsibilities despite the marquis' repeated requests. Finally, in an effort to force Jie to come out, the marquis set fire to the mountain forest, but Jie wouldn't leave his mountain retreat, and burned to death. From that time on, people abstained from using fire on the day of Jie's death and ate only cold food.

Ancestors: The Living Past

The grave offerings and geomantic arrangement of the tomb are designed to keep ancestors content and in good humor. These tasks are an integral aspect of ancestor worship—a belief which is at the heart of traditional Chinese religion and culture. In China, ancestor worship is an act of veneration, honor, and obligation. People venerate their deceased relatives because they have an obligation to care for their souls who now live in a shadowy afterworld. Ancestors are treated like living beings, who although dead, are still believed to have rights and duties.

According to the rules of ancestor worship, men venerate their parents and paternal grandparents, women venerate their father's side before marriage and their husband's after marriage. Individuals who contributed indirectly to the family and people who died unmarried or as children are also venerated, but they occupy a class apart from the true heads of the family.

Paper offerings and food for a deceased relative (Taiwan).

Neglect of paying proper respect will displease an ancestor, who will then punish his descendents like naughty children. Ancestors, however, says anthropologist Arthur Wolf, cannot cause major catastrophes, especially outside the realm of the family, because they are simply not powerful enough. Likewise, one cannot expect as much assistance from a plea to one's ancestor as from a god because an ancestor commands less authority. Ancestors have even been known to ignore requests, but they cannot brush aside repeated solicitations. If they do, the descendent can abandon filial obligation, leaving the ancestor to fend for himself, scurrying for food outside the back door with the despised class of wandering ghosts.

Ancestor worship is not dying out—younger generations show no indication of forsaking this practice. These days, even those modern urban Chinese who have abandoned the belief that ancestors actually need the livings' offerings continue the practice, for to abandon these commemorative rites makes most families feel uncomfortable. There is, after all, a sense of peace, continuity, and belonging when one remembers a favorite grandmother, a sympathetic aunt or an indulgent uncle through family ritual. Moreover, ancestor worship symbolizes the head of the family's devotion to his descent line and, if he too has a family, such rites mark the end of his own childhood and pride in the beginning of a new generation.

Flights of Fancy

On Qingming day, after people visit family graves and pay respects to their ancestors, the day turns into a spring holiday with picnicking and games.

One of the most pleasant activities, where one can take advantage of favorable spring winds, is of course kite flying. Kites originated in China and were popular as a folk craft there long before spreading across the world. The first recorded mention of kites was made some 2,500 years ago during the Spring and Autumn Period (770–476 B.C.) and described the fabrication of a kite which imitated the form of sparrow hawks circling in the sky. Kites also had military applications for signaling and measuring distances to enemy fortifications.

Over the centuries kites have been fashioned into an imaginative variety of shapes and designs—sand swallows, geese, tadpoles, frogs, bats, crabs, cicadas, butterflies, and herons. Some kites illustrate plots from folk tales or historical legends such as the Monkey King in battle or Nezha stirring up the sea. Other designs convey auspicious wishes—there's Chang E, the moon goddess; the beautiful maiden He who grants immortality; or the lucky characters meaning "great prosperity fills the sky."

Chinese kites have also been ingeniously crafted to make sounds in the wind or special visual effects by the attachment of various accessories to the frames. During the Five Dynasties (907–960) Li Ye made a kite in the imperial palace and fixed bamboo pipes to it that made a sound like the *zheng,* an ancient stringed instrument. This is the origin of the common word for kite in Chinese: *fengzheng,* "wind-zither." Additional devices included gongs, drums, organs, whistles, blinking eyes, spirals, and a "feeder" or "hurrier" which races up and down the towline.

Today in China the Festival of Clear Brightness is still the occasion for flying kites and even for conducting international kite competitions. For example, the city of Weifang in Shandong Province sponsored a three-day exhibition of kite flying in 1985 that included participants from ten countries—Holland, West Germany, the United States, Thailand, New Zealand, France, Hong Kong, Singapore, Japan, and Italy. The foreign kites were aerodynamically exciting but the Chinese flew kites that were far more appealing to the eye and seemingly impossible to fly, like a beautiful peacock the size of a small pagoda, an extravagant floating archway with circling fish hanging from it, and a dragon kite so tiny that it could fit into a pocket matchbox.

How Songs From a Kite Won a War

Legend has it that during the warring between the states of Chu and Han (206–202 B.C.) Han Xin, a famous general, surrounded the Chu force led by the famous General Xiang Yu and devised a plan to rout the enemy. He spent a day and a night constructing a giant wooden kite for the great warrior Zhang Liang to ride in. Zhang Liang flew above the Chu encampment singing Chu songs. Hearing the songs, the soldiers were so saddened with thoughts of home that they dispersed and Xiang Yu was defeated.

—CHINESE ARTISTIC KITES, by Ha Kuiming and Ha Yiqi

Artistic kite illustrating the character "double happiness" and the legendary Monkey King (Beijing).

Feast of the Hungry Ghosts

(15th day, 7th moon)

Gui Jie

The second "Festival of the Dead" somewhat resembles All Soul's Day or Halloween—a time when ghosts and spirits arise, the night is aglow with lanterns, and children scramble for candies and treats. Celebrated on the 15th day of the seventh month, and called the "Feast of the Hungry Ghosts," it probably originated as a Buddhist rite of salvation for ancestors. It may also have been connected to a harvest festival, although today it is devoted only to those among the dead who are not one's ancestors. Unlike the Qingming Festival, which stresses *family* ghosts and ancestors, the Hungry Ghost Festival is intended to pacify the ghosts of strangers and the uncared-for dead.

This festival of the seventh moon, also known as "The Yulan Assembly" *(yulanhui)* or "The Passage of Universal Salvation" *(pudu)*, marks a transition for inhabitants of the world of shades from the status of threatening ghost to that of stable spirit—for the time being anyway. During this period, all ghosts are released from the confines of the underworld to enjoy a month of freedom which culminates on the 15th day with a special ghost-feeding ritual.

Ghosts

When people die, their soul or *hun* lives in the world of darkness *(yinjian)*. If there are descendents to care for them, they will lead a comfortable afterlife. If there is no one to care for them, they turn into desperate ghosts *(gui)*. There is a continuum of obligation, as Arthur Wolf writes, marked on one end by honored, loved souls—the ancestors—and on the other end by miserable, abandoned strangers—the ghosts.

Different types of spirit money, some used for ghost encounters.

Dealing with ghosts is like dealing with gangs and bandits, bullies and beggars. These discontented souls include those who have no one to care for them because they died without descendents, or in childhood, or they perished far away from their families. More frightening, however, are the malicious ghosts who died before their time either as murder victims or suicides. They haunt the scene of their death seeking revenge. This varied assemblage of despairing beings is euphemistically referred to as "good brethren" *(hauxiongdi),* and the only way to avoid their mischievous doings and wrathful hate is to offer sacrifices to them, essentially to buy them off. But just as families do not invite beggars inside the house, these dismal souls are not encouraged to enter, and sacrifices to them are made outside the home.

The Ceremony

Taoist priest performing rites for the Hungry Ghost Festival (Tainan, Taiwan).

During the seventh month the gates of the underworld are opened and all souls suffering in the nether regions are free to wander wherever they like. Throughout this period, families perform private rituals outside their home with offerings of gifts and food to placate these unfortunate souls. On the 15th day a large community celebration takes place in which Buddhist and Taoist priests chant liturgies, perform rituals on an outdoor altar, and offer incense, paper clothes, and "spirit money" to the ghosts. [See color plate 4b.] The ceremony comes to a climax when the priest tosses buns and candy to hungry ghosts. The watching crowd (usually children) all rush to gather up the long-awaited sweets. In some cases though, the crowd can become quite unruly. There have even been incidents where rampaging middle-aged women pushed and shoved for snatches of festival treats, behaving like the very ghosts whose violent behavior the rites were meant to assuage.

There are a number of ceremonies—musical performances, invitations to the gods to attend the ritual, and the release of water lanterns (discussed later)—that occur before the actual ghost-feeding festival. In a small rural community in northern Taiwan, the feeding doesn't happen until a day and a half after the onset of the festival, around lunchtime on the 17th day. A crowd begins to gather at the temple to watch the afternoon's entertainment of opera. Then, the ceremony begins when the chief priest directs his assistants and musicians to usher the ghosts into the temple. One author has described the lively ritual:

> Accompanied by gongs, drums and double-reeded shawms, the priests read sutras and perform mudras (esoteric hand signs) that purify the altar area in front of the temple. The priests and musicians then climb up to the altar table, which is raised about a meter off the ground . . . the chief priest sits in a cross-legged, meditative posture on a platform just behind the altar table. . . he installs five powerful deities in a crown that he then mounts on top of his ordinary hat. He thus becomes the personification of the deities . . . he invites a series of Buddhas and Bodhisattvas (or gods for the Taoists) to the ceremony, and then invites the ghosts in a long passage that describes their sufferings in flowery detail. The priest now becomes a merciful deity associated with aid for ghosts; this is Guanyin for the Buddhists, and the Great Unity Heavenly Worthy Who Relieves Suffering for the Taoists. In this form, the priest transforms the plates of buns and candy on the altar table into quantities enormous enough to feed the starving crowd of ghosts; the offerings brought by the community could never be enough to sate the mob of ghosts. Meanwhile the priest and his assistants describe the miserable conditions of the ghosts' lives and preach to them. This is the point at which the food is thrown out to the hungry ghosts and snatched up by the waiting people. At the end of the two- or three-hour ceremony, the priest sends newly reformed ghosts to the heavenly Buddhist Pure Land, where they are released from their ghostly status; he returns the unreformed ghosts back to their sufferings in the underworld.

—Unities and Diversities in Chinese Religion, by Robert P. Weller

Offerings of red buns and cakes (Tainan County, Taiwan).

In most areas, ghosts are dealt with outside the temple or home, or by graveside altars. Individual families offer them raw and uncooked rice, raw noodles, unpeeled fruit, and uncut meats, similar to the dishes offered at an ancestor's outdoor gravesite.

Material gifts include stacks of paper, ingots, and spirit money, as well as small paper suits of clothing and jewelry. These offerings to vagabond ghosts, although ample, don't begin to compare to the fantastic collection of paper miniatures offered to ancestors. On display during funerals and commemorative services, there are multi-story foil mansions replete with cars, servants, lawn furniture, televisions, and rice pots. The houses are delicately assembled with bamboo splits and colored paper, some standing as high as five feet, with curved roofs and mirrored walls. This paper world is a unique art form, with skilled craftsmen able to produce surprisingly realistic but ephemeral settings which must be entirely burned to be properly "transferred" to the ghostly realm of needy spectres.

Family offerings to hungry ghosts (Tainan County, Taiwan).

Release of the Water Lanterns

On the evening before the Ghost Festival, there is a lovely custom celebrated in areas of Hong Kong and Taiwan, of sending beautifully decorated paper boats and water lanterns downstream in a rite called "Release of the Water Lanterns" *(fangshuideng)*. In customs chronicled in the 1920s, paper boats were filled with paper crews of underworld divinities. Lotus-flower lanterns were launched on the waterways with candles fixed on them to light the way for wandering ghosts. Priests conducted ceremonies on the river banks to invoke the gods' blessings and invite the souls of the drowned as guests of honor in the next day's feast. Where there were no creeks or rivers nearby, children would parade the streets holding lanterns and chanting rhyming couplets for the benefit of the visiting ghosts and their spirit-wary hosts. Although not practiced in the People's Republic of China today, this previously was a widespread event in many of the coastal provinces of pre-revolutionary China.

Stacks of ritual paper money (Taiwan).

Grandfather Seven and Grandfather Eight

Grandfather Seven (Qi Ye) and Grandfather Eight (Ba Ye) are two famous spirits who occupy a position in the godly bureaucracy as "patrolmen," reporting neighborhood misconduct to the City God.

Grandfather Eight, depicted as a short, stout, black figure with rolling eyes, is just the opposite of Grandfather Seven, who stands very tall and is very thin with a long, lolling red tongue. Legend has it that during their mortal life they were devoted friends. One day they scheduled an afternoon meeting but, as fate would have it, Grandfather Eight was caught in a torrential rainstorm and drowned in a nearby river (turning him black). When Grandfather Seven found Grandfather Eight, he was so overcome with grief that he hung himself (thereby acquiring a long tongue). As a reward for their loyalty to each other, they were granted the position of guardsmen, and very large, puppetlike representations of them can be seen parading through their local districts, especially in Taiwan, on festival days.

A workshop where paper houses are made for the dead (Taiwan).

A Ghost Story
Sung Ting-po (Song Dingbo) Catches a Ghost

Sung Ting-po of Nanyang, when a young man, met a ghost one night as he was walking.
"Who are you?" he asked.

The ghost answered, "A ghost." It then asked, "And who are you?"

"I am a ghost too," lied Sung.

"Where are you going?"

"To the town of Wan," was the reply.

"So am I."

They went along together for several *li*.

"Walking like this is too slow. Why not carry each other in turn?" suggested the ghost.

"A good idea," agreed Sung.

First the ghost carried him for several *li*.

"How heavy you are!" said the ghost. "Are you really a phantom?"

"I am a new ghost," answered Sung. "That's why I am heavy."

Then he carried the ghost, who was no weight at all. And so they went on, changing several times.

"As I am a new ghost," remarked Sung presently, "I don't know what we spectres have to fear most."

"What we detest is men's spittle."

They proceeded together till they came to a stream. Sung invited the ghost to cross first, which it did without a sound. Sung, however, made quite a splash.

"How comes it that you make such a noise?" inquired the ghost.

"That's because I am a new ghost. I am not accustomed yet to wading through water. You mustn't blame me."

As they approached the town of Wan, Sung threw the ghost over his shoulder and held it fast. With a screech the ghost begged to be put down, but Sung paid no attention, making straight for the town. When he set the ghost down, it had turned into a sheep. He promptly sold it, having spat at it first to prevent it from changing into another form. Then he left, the richer by one thousand five hundred coins.

Shih Chung (Shi Zhong) commented on this at the time as follows:

Sung Ting-po did better than most,
Made fifteen hundred coins by selling a ghost.

—STORIES ABOUT NOT BEING AFRAID OF GHOSTS (translated by Yang Hsien-yi and Gladys Yang)

Visions of the Underworld

In Chinese popular belief, the soul after death is judged according to the number of good deeds and bad deeds performed during its lifetime. If its evil actions outweigh the meritorious (and they usually do), the soul must proceed through the 10 tribunals of hell. The underworld courts, which are individually designed to handle specific crimes, operate like small cities—each realm has its own administrative staff and a specialized geography crowded with towers, cells, ponds, and prisons for punishing the condemned.

The complex sets of the underworld theater, however, took time to develop, just as they did in popular Christianity in the West. Early pictorial representations of hell show only a hint of the elaborate detail of later paintings. Hell scrolls from the Song and Yuan dynasties focus more on the stark drama of underworld confrontations than on elaborate descriptions of its scenery and operations. In these early scrolls the viewer sees the judge and several muscle-flexing demons attending to one or two transgressors writhing in repentance—each scene is vivid and immediate, the personal terror unrestrained and convincing.

Contemporary portrayals of Chinese Hell, Chambers Three and Seven (Taiwan).

In contrast, 19th- and 20th-century paintings depict underworld magistrates with increased responsibilities and chambers overflowing with prisoners and jailers. The ambience takes on the air of a sinister three-ring circus. Judges are overshadowed by their numerous scribes, attendants, secretaries, and torturers, while the raw terror is administered within a contrasting lull of bureaucratic efficiency.

The new look of hell accommodated a burgeoning range of wrongdoings. Categories of moral transgressions began to stress the social precepts of Confucianism over the religious tenets of Buddhism. The picture frame was filled with prisoners on trial for adultery, refusing to pay taxes, and ignoring the duties of filial piety.

The structure and command of underworld law and order remained the same from early times on, but otherworldly punishments were no longer restricted to cangues and shackles. Artists developed a visual repertoire consisting of such tortures as death by tongue-pulling, grinding, and pounding, or banishment to the mountain of swords, the pit of fire, and the cauldron of boiling oil. Vignettes of confrontations beyond the grave drawn from folklore and legend were interspersed throughout the underworld stage with scenes showing activities by which a sinner could redeem his or her sins. More than ever the underworld seemed to require guide books (called *shanshu*) for explaining the specialized "divisions" of hell which were designed to frighten people into leading moral lives.

A Journey Through Hell

The most popular myth connected with the Hungry Ghost Festival is the Buddhist story of "Mulian Saving His Mother from Hell." During the Tang dynasty (618–907), earlier versions of this tale were greatly elaborated by professional storytellers near Buddhist temples, where people would gather around to enjoy the festivities, listen to poems, and gaze at illustrations depicting favorite legends and folktales from the popular tradition. The Mulian story, which is filled with adventurous rescue attempts and terrifying descriptions of the underworld, excelled in entertainment value. It was the Buddhist equivalent of *Raiders of the Lost Ark*.

The protagonist of the story, Mulian, a disciple of Sakyamuni and a practitioner of powerful magic, is a devout Buddhist monk who makes a harrowing journey through the underworld in search of his mother,

Qingti. The various gods that he meets along the way—King Yama (Yenlo Wang), the Generals of the Five Paths, and numerous wardens—don't seem to know where she is located, so he must descend deeper and deeper into the inferno. He sees oxhead and horseface jailers with "teeth like jagged stumps." He passes through noxious vapors and the black fires of hell. Finally, he discovers his mother in the last and deepest of hells, the Avici hell. Here, the condemned go through continuing cycles of suffering, death and rebirth, without any pause and without any rest.

Before Mulian can embrace his mother, a guard pulls 49 spikes out of her body and, at last, they are reunited. After a short visit, Qingti is driven back into her cell, and Mulian leaps into the sky to tell the Buddha all about his sorrow and suffering. At this point, the Buddha releases the inhabitants of the Avici hell, who are all reborn in heaven. Unfortunately, Qingti's sins are too great and she is reborn as a hungry ghost. Her suffering is indeed bitter:

> The throat feels like the tiny aperture of a needle, so small that water cannot drip through, while the head is like the T'ai (Tai) Mountains, which [the waters of] three rivers are not enough to cover. Without one's even hearing so much as a hint of water and drink, the months go by, the years pass, and the miseries of starvation must be endured. From a distance, pure, cool, refreshing waters can be seen, but up close, they turn into a pus flow. Delicious food, delectable meals, turn into blazing fire.[1]

Mulian begs in the heavens for food to share with his mother and all the other hungry ghosts. But when Qingti sees the food her son has brought her, her stinginess and greed prevent her from giving any to her companions. She uses one hand to cover up the bowl and the other to scoop out the food, but before the food reaches her mouth it turns into a raging flame.

Gradually Qingti atones for her wrongdoings and moves upward on the path of rebirth, one step at a time. The *Yulanhui* Ghost Festival was instituted to help Mulian's mother secure her place in paradise. The story concludes with Qingti being spirited away by celestial acoyltes and dragons to the Land of Buddha and everlasting bliss. Henceforth, on the 15th day of the seventh month, monks and nuns chant the *yulanpen* sutra to rescue the ancestors from the fate of underworld punishment.

FESTIVALS OF ROMANCE AND COMPASSION, SURVIVAL AND MARRIAGE

Festival of the Cowherd and Weaving Maiden
(7th day, 7th moon)
Qixi Jie

On the seventh day of the seventh month, romance fills the air as the cowherd and weaving maiden celebrate their annual tryst through the star-laden heavens.

According to legend, the Emperor of Heaven had a beautiful daughter well skilled in the art of weaving. One day she and her six sisters descended to earth to bathe in a stream near a green pasture. A cowherd happened to see them and became entranced with the beauty of the weaving maiden. He snatched away her clothes and took them home with him. This prevented the weaving maiden from leaving earth to return to the sky. When the celestial weaving maiden discovered who was behind this prank and met the cowherd, she fell deeply in love with him and they married. [See color plate 6b.]

They lived happily for several years and were so enamored with each other that the maiden stopped spinning altogether and the cowherd forgot to tend to his cows.

The Queen Mother of the West became quite upset with this state of affairs and commanded the weaving maiden to return to Heaven. The maiden found her original clothes and flew off to the sky. The cowherd attempted to follow, but before he could reach his beloved, the Queen Mother took a golden hairpin from her hair and with it drew a great river (known as the Milky Way) between them. The weaving maiden now sits on one side of the river and is identified with Vega and Lyra. The herdsman sits on the other side and is identified with the constellation Aquila.

The two lovers are allowed to meet only once a year on the seventh night of the seventh month. At that time, flocks of magpies fly together to form a bridge so that the maiden can cross the river and be reunited with her husband.

But if there is rain on this day, the river will flood and sweep away the bridge, thus preventing their long-awaited meeting. However, there is another version in which the presence of rain is taken to mean that they have actually met and that the droplets are, in fact, the tears of the separating couple, who must wait another full year before their tender rendezvous.

Poem of the Herd-Boy and Maiden

Distant and faint the Herd-Boy Star,
Bright and lustrous the Heavenly River Maid;
Gently plying her slender white hands,
Cha-cha hum her shuttle and loom.
Day after day, her pattern unfinished,
Her tears fall in droplets like rain.
The Heavenly River, shallow and clear,
Divides them now by only a space;
Lovely and tender, with the river between,
Longingly, they look but cannot speak.

—Anonymous poet, fifth or sixth century A.D., from SUNFLOWER SPLENDOR (translated by Dell R. Hales)

A Women's Ceremony

The Weaving Maiden is traditionally considered a patron spirit of women's work, and the festival, like the Mid-Autumn moon festival, is mainly a women's celebration.

Unmarried girls make offerings consisting of paper imitations of combs, mirrors, flowers, and rouge-pots arranged in sets of seven, one for the Weaving Maiden and one for each of her six sisters. There are also seven bowls of fruit filled with different types of melons and seven sets of sewing articles: needles, threads, scissors, and so on.

Traditionally, contests were held to see who could thread needles the fastest in a darkened room with no more light than the glow of a burning ember or pale moonlight (there is only a half moon on Double Seven—the seventh day of the seventh month).

Divination methods were practiced to determine one's dexterity in needlework. In some areas of Fujian women put spiders in boxes and if they wove well-shaped webs the following day, the women were assured of their talent in weaving and sewing. In Beijing, girls would set a bowl of water outdoors and float a small needle in it. If the shadow cast was thin like a thread, the girl would be skillful at needlework, if it was thick like a stick, she would be clumsy. (In some areas, bean sprouts were substituted for needles.)

Today, according to Joan Law and Barbara Ward, whose photo-documentary covers festivals in Hong Kong in the 1980s, girls often "club together" to assemble grand displays of women's toiletries in honor of the seven maidens.

Collective wedding (contemporary Chinese folk painting).

Tian Hou, Protectress of Seafarers
(23rd day, 3rd moon)

The 23rd day of the third month is celebrated as the birthday of Tian Hou, the compassionate and omniscient Goddess of the Sea. More affectionately called Mazu or "Grandmother," she is especially popular among seafaring communities in Zhejiang, Fujian, Guangzhou, and Taiwan. Tian Hou is the second most popular deity in Taiwan (the most popular being the Buddhist Goddess of Mercy, Guanyin). Mazu was also widely worshiped by early Chinese immigrants to California, probably for protection on the dangerous sea passage between China and North America.

A Taiwanese painting of Mazu.

Queen of Heaven

Most hagiographies agree that Mazu was born on the island of Meizhou off the coast of Fujian Province in the 10th century, and that her family name was Lin. A maiden who never married, she possessed great supernatural powers and could, according to popular belief, rescue sea travelers from perilous storms. When still a child, while asleep and dreaming in her home, it was said that she appeared to her brothers, who were in a boat caught in a storm at sea, and saved them from drowning.

In her representations on temple altars she has two assistants, the brothers Thousand-mile Eye (Qianli Yen) and Favorable Wind Ear (Shunfeng Er). They look like ferocious pirates, with flaming eyes, horns on their heads, scraggly beards, and razor-sharp teeth. Originally, Thousand-mile Eye and Favorable Wind Ear served a tyrant general and were later vanquished in a fierce battle. In the battles, soldiers waved hundreds of large flags and beat thousands of drums so the brothers could not use their divine powers to fight. After their defeat they became loyal servants of Mazu, using their abilities to help the goddess see and hear people in need of aid thousands of miles across the ocean.

Over the centuries there have been many stories describing Mazu's miracles, from how she saved shipwrecked ambassadors and protected lost mariners to the way she assisted Kublai Khan in expanding his control over coastal territories and aided Koxinga in the overthrow of the Dutch in Taiwan. She became a holy goddess in Ming dynasty times and was elevated to the rank of Queen of Heaven during the Qing dynasty. Mazu is honored as the patron goddess of sailors, benefactress to mothers in childbirth, and a controller of floods and droughts.

She is usually depicted as a plump, matronly woman, with a full and serene face, possessing the quiet dignity and regal air suited to her rank as Empress of Heaven.

Temple charm illustrating Mazu and her attendants (Taiwan).

China and the United States: Tian Hou in San Francisco

The oldest Chinese temple in the United States is dedicated to Mazu and is located in San Francisco's Chinatown. It was built in 1852 by the first wave of Chinese settlers to the West Coast. Mazu shares the temple with a host of other deities including Guan Di, Supporter of Heaven and Protector of the Kingdom; Jin Hua, Goddess of Women and Children, and her 12 attendants; Hua Guang, God of Wisdom; and Hua To, God of Medicine.

The temple is full of artifacts—pewter urns, tapestries, elaborately-designed altar tables, gilded trellis panels—that clearly show the skill of temple craftsmen. Many of these items were donated before 1911, the last year of dynastic rule in China. The temple is still very active today, especially during the New Year and on Mazu's birthday when groups of women can be seen busily arranging elaborate offerings and preparing stacks of gold-foil paper to be burned in honor of the Queen of Heaven.

Festival Day

On her festival day, Mazu is feted with opera performances and puppet shows. Priests chant before the altar to purify the community. Spirit mediums in touch with powerful deities go into trances. Bundles of spirit money and incense are burned in courtyards. People set out offerings of eggs, meat, buns, and cakes in front of the temple.

In Hong Kong, clubs known as "flower cannon societies" *(huapaohui),* gather at the temple and members scramble for numbered sticks hidden inside rockets shot from small cannons. The prizes, made by participating associations, are towering floral altars which bring good luck to the winners. They are numbered from one on up—the luckiest being number nine.

In Taiwan (where there are over 300 Mazu temples), numerous "daughter" Mazu images are carried in palanquins to visit "mother" Mazu in Beigang, the site of the oldest Mazu temple, established in 1730. Throughout the day, lion dancers, stilt walkers, acrobatic teams, and parade floats pass up and down the streets of Beigang. Busloads of people come from far and wide to visit the main temples and participate in all the festivities. Hotels are full, food stalls line the streets, vendors sell everything from pineapple cakes to salted fish, and souvenir stands are brimming over with banners, memorabilia, and toys. Firecrackers and fireworks displays more spectacular than those seen during the New Year are set off continuously through the night and into the next morning as a lasting tribute to Mazu's immense popularity on the island.

Celebrants at Mazu Festival (Taiwan).

Double Yang Day
(9th day, 9th moon)
(Chongyang Jie)

The ninth day of the ninth month seasonally marks the first chill of autumn and numerologically represents the symbol of *yang*—the positive, masculine force in Chinese cosmology. According to *yin-yang* duality, odd numbers are associated with the male principle, and the occurrence of two *yang* numerals, especially when they are both the number nine, is considered particularly advantageous—the overall message being good fortune and happiness for all.

This holiday is not as vigorously celebrated today as it once was. Its ancient roots are thought to lie in an autumnal version of an ancestor commemoration day, somewhat like the Clear Brightness Festival. The day of the double ninth has a dark side associated with fear, death, hills, high places, amulets, and magical herbs, and is even considered by some to be a "Festival of the Dead."

Hill Climbing and Chrysanthemum Parties

Today double Yang day is treated casually, and is not so widely observed as other holidays. It is also called "Mounting the Heights," and those who do celebrate it picnic on hillsides and drink chrysanthemum wine. A popular story from the Han dynasty explains the origin of this custom. It seems a famous practitioner of Taoist arts named Fei Changfang warned an honest and good-hearted friend, Huan Jing, of an impending disaster. Fei recommended that Huan pack some food and a jug of chrysanthemum wine and take his family to the shelter of a high hill. Huan did as he was told, and later that day, when he descended to his home, discovered his livestock all dead. He looked at his family and realized this would have been their fate had it not been for Fei's timely warning. To this day, chrysanthemum wine and hill-climbing have become a refreshing pastime to usher in the beginning of fall and commemorate the fortunate Huan Jing.

Double Yang day is also a time of chrysanthemum parties where viewers gather together to admire the late year blooms of the chrysanthemum, the flower of autumn noted also as a symbol of longevity and good health. It is considered one of the "four gentlemen of blossoms" together with the cymbidium, prunus, and bamboo.

Chrysanthemums have been cultivated in the gardens of flower fanciers for centuries, resulting in numerous varieties with many unusual and colorful names. The following list of selected stalks is gleaned from a 19th-century gentleman's index of special varieties:

snow-covered cinnabar
precious monastery of the spring dawn
goose-quills
white crane sleeping in the snow
purple tiger-whiskers
immortal's palms
golden Buddha seat
Heavenly Maid (i.e., Weaving Maiden)
scattering flowers
drunken Li Po (705?–762, one of China's greatest poets and noted for his love of wine)
eyebrows of the Old Ruler (i.e., the Taoist sage, Laozi)

—From ANNUAL CUSTOMS AND FESTIVALS IN PEKING (translated by Derk Bodde)

Chrysanthemums

Wine flows
by the east gate;
I pour against
the fading evening glow.

The dark fragrance
fills my empty sleeves;
Don't say the heart
is not broken.

The west wind
lifts the curtain,
and even the bending petals
of the yellow chrysanthemum
look more forceful
than my shadow.

—Li Qingzhao (translated and excerpted by the authors)

*The chrysanthemum,
which blooms in autumn,
has been the inspiration
for generations of poets
and artists in the East.*

FOUR

The Rites of Matrimony

Many of the elements of seasonal festivals—food, dance, fortunetelling and ritual—are also found in the celebrations of important events and passages in the cycle of individual and family life.

Among the celebrations of these events, the most richly colorful is the rite of matrimony. Like the sense of renewal that accompanies the onset of the New Year, the wedding also marks a time of great expectations, familial closeness, and new beginnings.

Our focus in this section is on the elaborate wedding ceremonies arranged for couples paired by village matchmakers, as observed mainly in Taiwan. The traditional way of meeting and becoming engaged through an intermediary is still practiced, especially in rural areas of Taiwan and the People's Republic, although communication, mutual attraction, and personal choice characterize a growing number of marriage decisions in present-day China.

Weddings today can range from simple civil ceremonies, where the bride and groom sign a marriage contract purchased at the corner stationer's shop, to long, complex betrothals with a dizzying array of nuptial rules to follow, symbolic gifts to bestow, and formal teas to attend. In all cases, however, there is more to the occasion than just being "joined together" as a married couple. In Chinese terms, the wedding ceremony is a statement to the ancestors of the groom's family that the family has brought in a daughter-in-law, a person who will help continue the descent line for another generation and aspire to preserve the integrity of her husband's household.

Finding the Right Man

My maternal grandparents or "outside grandmother" and "outside grandfather"—one of the words in maternal grandparents the same as in *foreigner* or *barbarian*—"outsiders" tracked BaBa down by following the invisible red string that ties his ankle to MaMa's. Year by year the string grew shorter.

The outside grandparents had four daughters, and so one of this grandmother's habits whenever she heard of an interesting boy or young man was to count him. Using the poor people's divining method, she took a pinchful of rice, said his name, and counted the grains to see if she had picked an odd or even number, carefully dropping each speck back into the rice box. Odd meant Yes, this boy was her daughter's true husband; even meant No, wrong boy; *four* sounds like *die*. In addition to counting rice, she confirmed the results by paying an expensive blind fortuneteller to touch a list of young men's names, and he picked out her future son-in-law. He also used the yarrow sticks and tortoise shell and told the wedding date.

—CHINA MEN, by Maxine Hong Kingston

Finding a Match

In old China, on the seventh day of the seventh moon [see color plate 6b], young Chinese girls presented the Weaving Maiden, patroness of unmarried girls, with numerous offerings and had their fortunes told in hope of receiving a favorable report on the type of man they would marry. Having little say in the matter of marriage, their fate rested in the hands of the Goddess of Matrimony and skillful matchmakers.

Today, in many rural communities, the matchmaker still plays a significant role in joining a young woman and young man together. If the girl is of marriageable age (somewhere between 18 and 23, although many young women, especially in urban areas, wait until they are in their late 20s or early 30s before considering marriage), her family is contacted by a matchmaker who sets up an initial meeting with the prospective groom (usually the groom's family takes the initiative in finding a bride and appointing the matchmaker). On this occasion the young girl presents tea to her guests. When she serves tea to the young man, she has her first awkward moment, the chance to look closely at him and size up her marital fate.

According to custom, if the young man approves of the young woman, he tentatively places a small embroidered red cloth bag on the saucer, and if she has a mutual feeling, she quickly accepts it. However, if she doesn't find him appealing, she leaves the room before he has a chance to present the bag. Nowadays, to avoid embarassment, young people give and take the bag regardless of their level of attraction—the only gauge for approval being the size of the pouch. In still other cases, especially in Taiwan, the "betrothal tea" is abandoned for chaperoned meetings held in the plush, mirrored interiors of city sweetshops and coffee houses.

Assuming the young people are interested in each other after a formal introduction, their Eight Characters—the year, month, day and hour of birth—are exchanged to see if they are compatible. The folklore of Chinese horoscopes has endured through countless generations, and fortunetellers today are still consulted in the hope of averting matrimonial disaster. What does the modern soothsayer look for? According to the rules of astrology, the most incompatible matches are signs on the astrological compass that are directly opposite each other and thus in conflict. Generally speaking, the worst relationships are made between the squabbling rat and restless horse, steadfast ox and whimsical ram, moody tiger and competitive monkey, brooding rabbit and forthright rooster, assertive dragon and proud dog, skeptical snake and carefree boar. For "marriages made in heaven," astrology experts suggest seeking out members within your "affinity group":

> rat, dragon, monkey—*ambitious and energetic*
> ox, snake, rooster—*purposeful and steadfast*
> tiger, horse, dog—*humanitarian and idealistic*
> rabbit, ram, pig—*emotional and artistic*

the idea being that similar personality traits guarantee an easygoing, harmonious relationship.

After a preliminary evaluation of the horoscope, the matchmaker sends the girl's Eight Characters to the prospective groom's house to be placed on the ancestral altar for three days. If no unfortuitous events occur, such as family illness or an object breaking, the young man's family will consider this a good omen and send their son's Eight Characters to the girl's family, who will follow the same procedure. Once the Eight Characters have been accepted by both sides, their dates are recorded together on one piece of red paper and the groom's family commissions a gold ring to be made for their son's future bride.

People today in their 70s and 80s still remember having their Eight Characters written and checked when they were very young children and, if the stars were favorable, becoming engaged to someone as early as age *five*. In the countryside it wasn't unusual for a boy to marry between seven and 10. His wife was usually older, between 12 and 18, and would for a time take care of him as an older sister would a younger brother. In wealthy families, however, it was common for the groom to be 10 or 20 years older than his young bride.

Engagement

The engagement becomes official with the presentation of the "12 betrothal gifts" by the groom's family to the bride and her family. In the countryside, many of these items consist of pairs of livestock: two ducks, two chickens, two lambs, two pigs, and so on. In urban areas, pairs of store-bought items such as shoes, handkerchiefs, and blouses are more common. In addition, sugar-coated wintermelon, tangerine tarts, pomegranates, silk-thread noodles (vermicelli), dried longan, and pagoda-shaped candies are sent, as well as gold bracelets and jewelry. The number of gifts would make any young bride smile with delight, but out of politeness the bride's family does not accept them all. To ensure the good luck of the male's family, the cocks (symbol of male vigor) are usually returned along with some of the other goods. Following the fine points of bridal etiquette, however, not enough items are returned to imply that the presents were in some way unacceptable.

While the groom's family is busily preparing engagement gifts, the bride's family reciprocates with 12 presents for him. Among these gifts are lanterns, incense and candles, firecrackers, wine, ham, deer horn (valued for its medicinal qualities and used as an aphrodisiac), and bird's nest (a Chinese delicacy used in soups). Like the bride's family, the groom's family accepts only some of the gifts, such as the lanterns and incense, and returns the rest. In some cases the bride's family sends a trunk full of theater costumes, and if the boy's family is in full accord with the wedding arrangements, they stage a small romantic folk opera accompanied by neighborhood musicians to celebrate the joyous occasion and thank the ancestors for their good fortune.

The engagement is announced to the bride's family and relatives by distributing "betrothal cakes," boxed and unboxed, that are provided by the groom's family. These delicate white cakes, which taste something like Danish butter cake, have a thin filling of sweet syrup and are topped with sesame seeds. The more elaborate boxed cakes imply that the recipient is expected to give a wedding present in return.

Finally, the most important of all the presents to the bride is the grand gift that comprises the formal request of marriage along with a substantial amount of money. It isn't unusual for a family to spend half its annual income on acquiring a bride. For a financially well-off family in Taiwan, even 20 to 30 years ago, the average amount of gift money was $2,500. For most economically successful families today, every effort is made by the parents to provide an adequate monetary foundation for launching the newly married couple's life together. This amount can be combined with the 12 gifts or given separately at a later date.

After the items are presented in front of the groom's ancestral shrine, the bride's family invites the groom's family to receive tea. As the bride offers sweet tea to the elders of her future husband's family, they place a red packet of money on the tea tray. When she has completed this part of the formal tea, the high point of the engagement ceremony begins.

The matchmaker seats the bride-to-be on a chair in the ancestral hall. If she is facing the door with her back to the home altar, this indicates she will be leaving her family for the groom's household; if, however, she is seated facing her father's ancestral table, this means the husband will be moving in with her.

Once the bride is seated, her future mother-in-law (not her fiancée—he isn't even present) places a golden ring on her finger. An auspicious wedding date is chosen according to the almanac, and the rest of the time (usually a year elapses between the engagement and the wedding) is spent accumulating a plentiful dowry and attending bridal showers.

Bridal Curses

Traditionally, the separation of a bride from her family was one of the most painful experiences a young woman could expect to face in her entire life. Never having been away from home, she could find marriage extremely lonely as she tried to please a demanding mother-in-law, fit into a new domestic routine with competitive sisters-in-law, and find time and energy to become acquainted with her newly-met husband.

The bride associates warmth, comfort and security with her father's house, and coldness, discomfort, and unease with the groom's house. To ventilate her anxious and often suppressed feelings, she is allowed to mourn the loss of her immediate family, revile the matchmaker, and scold the groom's side for three days before the wedding through "weeping songs" (*kuge*) or "marriage laments" *(hunge)*. This is a common bridal custom in such areas as Guangdong, Shanghai, Guangxi, and Hubei.[1]

Some of the verses are memorized, others are cued by sisters, relatives and friends, and sometimes the curses are spontaneously created by the bride, revealing her wit, drive, and personality. Crying and laughing, wailing and cursing, the bride likens her fate to impending death. The need for a bride to weep, however, is slowly diminishing as the modern woman has a greater voice in determining her future mate.

The Bride Sings, the Bride Weeps

On her third to the last evening at home, MaMa dressed in white. A lucky old woman, who had a good woman's long life, helped her wash her hair, though this being modern days she only sprinkled water on her head. Dressed in white, MaMa sat behind her bedcurtains to sing-and-weep. "Come and hear the bride cry," the village women invited one another. "Hurry. Hurry. The bride's started singing-and-crying." "Listen. Listen. The bride's singing. The bride's weeping." They sat around the bed to listen as if they were at the opera. The girl children sat too; they would learn the old and new songs. The women called out ideas: "Cry about the years your mother held you prisoner." "And you're ransomed at last." "Scold your mother for not finding you your husband sooner."

"Give me a rifle to shoot my mother down," MaMa wailed. "Mother, you've kept me working at your house. You've hidden me from my husband and family. Mother, I'm leaving you now. I'm aiming my rifle at your stomach and shooting you down."

"Oh-h-h," exclaimed the women. "She's the best crying bride I've ever heard." The drummers banged. The bride's mother stood against the wall and smiled proudly....

The women punctuated her long complaints with clangs of pot lids for cymbals. The rhymes made them laugh. MaMa wailed, her eyes wet, and sang as she laughed and cried, mourned, joked, praised, found the appropriate old songs and invented new songs in melismata of singing and keening. She sang for three evenings. The length of her laments that ended in sobs and laughter was wonderful to hear.

—China Men, by Maxine Hong Kingston

The Wedding

Three days prior to the wedding, the dowry is transported on a lengthy line of carts, something like a betrothal float, to the groom's home. The bride's clothing, household furnishings, domestic linens, and gifts of money are elaborately and openly presented on each cart for all passersby to see and admire.

Taking Leave, Seclusion, and Arrival

On the day of the wedding, the nervous bride begins the final stage of preparation for her new identity as she transforms herself from filial daughter to devoted wife.

The bride bathes and puts on the layers of her wedding dress. Traditionally, the inner garments were white and were meant to be later used as her funerary garments. The outer garment included an embroidered red skirt that would be remade into baby clothes for her first child. Her hair would be adorned with tinkling ornaments, kingfisher jewelry, and golden arrow hairpins (to fend off malign spirits). Today, however, most brides in Taiwan and Hong Kong forgo the traditional look for a Western-style white gown which is rented or purchased just for the occasion—they will also rent the traditional costume for wedding photographs.

A veil concealing her features, the bride is lifted into the red sedan chair. Brass gongs are clanged to hasten her entrance into the sedan chair (today it's more common to use a taxi). If she lingers too long between the door of her home and the door of her nuptial carriage, her good energy will likely remain at home and the wealth of the family will escape through the door.

As she ascends, an umbrella or rice-winnowing basket is held over her head so she will not be observed from heaven in this liminal state. A great deal of weeping and hugging between the bride and her mother occurs at this emotional moment as she begins the journey away from her parent's household.

In old times, green bamboo was used to support the bridal sedan chair to symbolize the purity of the bride. If the bamboo still had leaves showing, this signified the long life of the bride's relatives. The bridal procession was led by the matchmaker and followed by the groom's assistants, the younger brothers of the bride and bridegroom, musicians, and lantern bearers. (Today, everyone crowds into a fleet of taxis.) As the procession moved slowly through the streets to the groom's home, the bride would toss wintermelon candies out of the palanquin to symbolize the abandonment of her bad habits. And if by chance the bridal parade met another, the matchmakers exchanged paper flowers to avoid canceling out each other's good fortune.

Strings of firecrackers are set off when the procession arrives at the groom's home. As the bride descends, lucky phrases are spoken and a variety of symbolic rituals may be performed. Sometimes a basin of smoldering coals is set before the bridal chair to consume any bad spirits that may have traveled with the bride. Splashed with a cup of wine, the basin ignites in brilliant flames to symbolize the prosperous life expected of the newly paired couple. The bridegroom shoots several arrows into the sky to chase off any lingering ghosts and then the bride descends from the sedan chair holding an apple or a vase. These two objects are selected because they rhyme with the first syllable of the word "tranquility" *(ping)*. She may be asked to step over a saddle as well, since that item sounds the same as the second syllable of "tranquility" *(an)*. An embroidered cloth with the eight trigrams and *yin-yang* symbol is hung up to dispel any ill fortune.

The eight trigrams surrounding a Yin/Yang symbol, the essence of creation.

New Identity

A young boy presents tangerines symbolizing good fortune to welcome the new bride, and an old woman who is a friend of the family and whose life has been filled with luck escorts her through the groom's house. The reception room is decorated with bright red hangings containing the double characters for "happiness" *(xi)* in gold lettering and painted scrolls of the Twin Gods of Mirth and Harmony, He He Erxian, the connotation being "two in body, but one in spirit."

The bride and groom bow three times to the ancestral shrine in the main hall and then enter the newlywed room. Here, they drink from goblets tied together by a red ribbon and then, crossing arms, they exchange the cups and drink again. After eating a light repast of "sons-and-grandsons" cakes and longevity noodles, they prepare for the evening banquet.

The bride changes into a red satin evening gown for the wedding feast, her arms covered with gold and jade bracelets. All of the groom's relatives seat themselves according to rank to view the young couple. The groom is expected to toast each guest and the bride offers tea and candy as a means of introduction, receiving in return the ubiquitous red bags filled with gifts of money.

After the feasting is over and the bride and groom prepare for the wedding night, they are subjected to a seemingly endless barrage of lascivious jokes and sayings about fertility, procreation, and the new bride's virginity (which is still not totally uncommon, especially among young women who have few opportunities for unchaperoned dates). In the old days all rules of etiquette and propriety were suspended for three days in a custom referred to as "bringing down the newlyweds' bedroom." If the men were too boisterous and rowdy in their comments, the bride's family would jump in and reprimand them. The next day, the bedsheets or the bride's undergarments were checked to report on their nuptial success.

Having endured to this point, the bride eagerly awaits the third day of the marriage, when she and her husband visit her parents' household. On the 10th day she again makes a visit to her family, but this time alone, regarded now as a newly married woman, a member of another family.

The Twin Gods He He holding their attributes—a box (pronounced "he") and a lotus (also pronounced "he")—a favorite motif for weddings because the word "he" is homophonous with "harmony."

Visit to the bride's home, three days after the wedding (contemporary Chinese folk painting).

Rats' Wedding Day

A popular folk custom in China concerns the rats' wedding procession. Around the New Year holiday, children were told that if they went to bed early and were very quiet, they might hear the sounds of the rats' wedding party. Rats and mice were not welcome guests in a home—increasing numbers of them suggested the approaching dilapidation of a household. Therefore, New Year prints of the rats' wedding were hung in the home, probably as a kind of talisman to ensure that these annoying creatures would eventually leave.

Rats were left undisturbed only a few days out of the year (usually the third day of the 12th month, the seventh of the 12th, or the 19th of the first) so, as folklore claims, they could get married without interruption. If the wedding proceeded without a hitch, the grateful rats would not pester the inhabitants of the household for the remainder of the year. [See color plate 9a.]

Images of the wedding processions are very charming, showing the rat bride and groom with a host of attendants accompanying them—musicians, lantern-bearers, gong-beaters and palanquin carriers. Sometimes a cat about to pounce on a rat appears in the print—an effective magical image that might drive the rats from the household. The presence of the cat also figures prominently in a folktale where the cat is selected over the sun, clouds, wind, and wall as the bridegroom. In the end, the cat reigns supreme by eating his new bride.

Symbolic Foods

Roast Pig—In Guangdong and Hubei Province, a succulent offering of roast pig was sent to the bride's family on the third day after a wedding as a sign of the groom's family's acceptance and pleasure with their new daughter-in-law.

Wild Goose—A wild goose is the quintessential symbol of marital harmony and fidelity. Because geese mate for life and migrate together from season to season, they are considered dependable, reliable creatures. Pictures of wild geese flying in pairs make very appropriate wedding presents. If wild geese cannot be obtained for a betrothal gift, domestic geese are permissable or even, as a last resort, humble chickens will do.

Egg Soup—On the day of the wedding, the groom is cordially served a bowl of soup upon his arrival at the bride's home. It contains an unbroken soft-boiled egg which he is expected to break to symbolize the bride's leave-taking from her family. Sometimes the groom's mother-in-law will put a hard-boiled egg in the soup, making him try a little harder to break the yolk in order to gain his bride.

Pig's Heart—The bride packages together a pig's heart along with other ingredients to make a soup for her in-laws on the day of the wedding to suggest that they are "all of one heart."

Fruits and Nuts—Because a wealth of puns can be made from Chinese names for fruits and nuts, they are symbolically used during the wedding ceremony to imply many children and good fortune. For example, folded inside the marriage quilt, one might find peanuts, dates and nuts—the second syllable in the word for peanut is *sheng*, which is homophonous with the word "birth" and the word for date *(zaozi)* sounds the same as the "early arrival of a male son." For the same reason, when the bride is presented in the main hall to her mother-in-law, she may be offered a plate of dates and chestnuts with a cup of fragrant tea.

Tea—A gift of tea (once an expensive commodity) was highly regarded in China's past, thus it was often used as an engagement present for the bride-to-be. Today, accepting the "gift of tea" is synonymous with the term for engagement.

The Last Emperor's Strange Wedding Night

Puyi (1906–1967), the last emperor of the Manchu dynasty, selected his bride from a photograph. The wedding lasted five days, with three days of theater performances and the bestowing of new titles. The procession included guards and cavalrymen, 72 dragon-and-phoenix umbrellas and flags and 30 pairs of imperial lanterns. The wedding presents ranged from silks and satins, cloisonné vases and porcelain dinnerware to ornate carpets with dragon-and-phoenix designs and beautiful scrolls wishing long life and good fortune.

The wedding night was spent in the Palace of Eastern Tranquility which according to Puyi "was a rather peculiar room: it was unfurnished except for the bed-platform which filled a quarter of it, and everything about it except the floor was red. When we had drunk the nuptial cup and eaten sons-and-grandsons cakes and entered this dark room I felt stifled. The bride sat down on the bed, her head bent down. I looked around me and saw that everything was red: red bed-curtains, red pillows, a red dress, a red skirt, red flowers and a red face . . . it all looked like a melted red wax candle. I did not know whether to stand or sit, decided that I preferred the Mind Nurture Palace, and went back there."

—EMPEROR TO CITIZEN, by Pu Yi (translated by W. J. F. Jenner)

Marriages in Hell

Trapping a husband for a young girl takes on an entirely different connotation when the bride-to-be is a ghost.[2] According to popular belief, such spirit unions occurred because a girl who died in childhood decides some years later that she needs a husband to give her children. Her "children," who are the living man's offspring from a real marriage, are then obliged to worship the ghost as their mother, providing it with offerings as though she had actually married when alive.

Such arranged spirit marriages assure that the dead girl's soul won't bring misfortune to her natal family or siblings' families, because she is now cared for and happy. Such a marriage also allows the bride's ancestral tablet to have a place of honor in her "husband's" household rather than a secluded position on her father's altar where she would be put if she had no descendents.

Sometimes the girl's spirit will alert her parents to her desire for marriage by appearing in a dream or by causing some mysterious sickness that can't seem to be cured by ordinary methods. A trance medium will then be consulted to diagnose the problem. When the family realizes the urgency of their daughter's request they'll try anything to find her a husband. One cunning method for a speedy betrothal is to place on a road a money purse containing the girl's name and horoscope. The first unsuspecting male passerby (married or unmarried—it doesn't matter) to pick up the purse is designated by the family as the dead girl's groom. Usually, the promise of a sizable dowry induces the man to readily agree to the marriage.

The marriage mimics an ordinary wedding in almost every detail, complete with a representation of a smiling bride. The girl's ancestral tablet is transformed into a doll bride. First, it is padded into the form of a figure with arms and legs, then dressed in a miniature wedding gown, ornamented with gold-colored bracelets and pendants and, as a finishing touch, topped off with the face of some beautiful cover girl cut out from a magazine.

Engagement gifts consist of wedding cakes and money, and the dowry includes boxes of fabric, clothing, and jewelry that the groom's living wife (if he is married) can use. Feasts are held at the bride's home and the groom's home. On the day of the wedding, the dressed "bride" sits in the family room of her home with her back to the altar. Upon leaving, the bride's brother escorts her to the taxi-cab which takes her to the groom's house. The tablet is placed in a chair next to the groom during the feasting and is later placed in the bedroom on the wedding night. The next morning it is positioned on the groom's family altar, its final resting place, where it will occupy a position of authority and respect for generations to come.

This custom has been reported as slowly dying out, but in some locations spirit marriages were still fairly common in the late 1960s and continue to be "celebrated," though less than in the past.

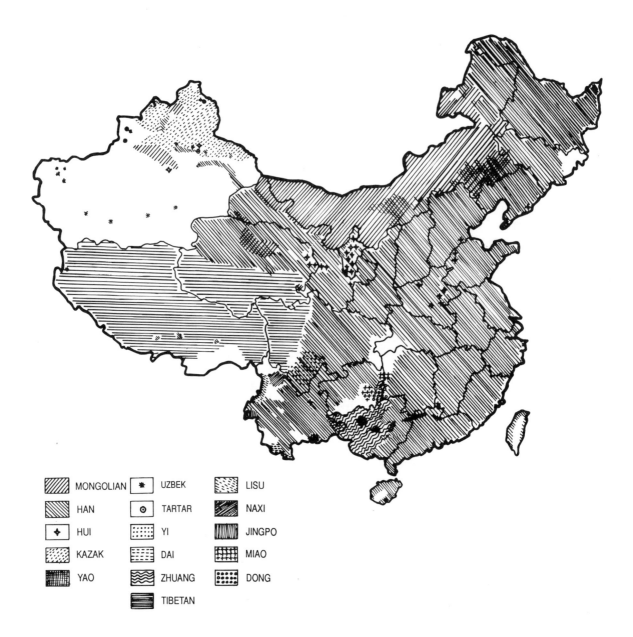

MONGOLIAN	UZBEK	LISU
HAN	TARTAR	NAXI
HUI	YI	JINGPO
KAZAK	DAI	MIAO
YAO	ZHUANG	DONG
	TIBETAN	

Festivals of Earth, Water, Wind, and Fire

National Minorities of China

When we look at the exciting mix of festivals celebrated by the billion people of China, we tend to think of all those who celebrate them as one ethnic group, the Han. The English term "Chinese," however, combines two very different definitions which should be kept quite distinct: politically, "Chinese" refers to anyone who is a citizen of the People's Republic of China; ethnically, it refers to someone who is a Han. The Han ethnic group, the largest in China, is named after the famous Han dynasty (206 B.C.–A.D. 220) and accounts for over 90% of the country's population.

There are, however, 55 other officially recognized ethnic groups constituting less than 10% of the population but occupying 50 to 60% of the country's total land area. The government officially refers to these ethnic groups as "National Minorities."

Many of the minority areas are located in the inhospitable desert and mountain ranges of northern, northeastern, and western China, a vast wide-open elevated region whose people are mostly Mongolian, Turkic or Tibetan, and in the southwestern regions.

For centuries, some of these non-Han groups have been cut off from the Han population by the world's largest man-made barricade—the Great Wall. Built in successive stages over the course of many dynastic rules, from the first millenium B.C. through to the 16th century A.D. (what we see today was built during the Ming dynasty), the wall separated tradi-

tionally agricultural from non-agricultural areas, distinguishing the northern Chinese plain and rich Yangtse River valley from grass-covered steppes, virgin swamps, and desolate mountain ranges—and isolating the warring "barbarians" from the "civilized" Han.

Politically, China proper (where the core of Han culture and settlement began in the middle of the Yellow River valley) and frontier areas of China were brought together under the Qing dynasty, mostly during the 18th century. Incursions by earlier dynasties into Xinjiang, Inner Mongolia and southern Manchuria did occur, but were later reversed. It is this latest process of expansion that accounts for the enormous size of the People's Republic of China today.

The lands comprising the frontiers of China are divided into five "autonomous regions": Inner Mongolia, Ningxia (Hui), Xinjiang (Uygur), Guangxi (Zhuang), and Tibet. To this should be added the smaller autonomous districts in China proper which are inhabited by minorities living in seemingly more "accessible" provinces such as Yunnan and Guizhou.

In the areas of China proper within the southwest and in the lower West River valley, unfavorable land barriers—broken hills, mountain country, and uneven land—prevented easy communication, and distinct non-Han ethnic groups flourished. Traces of these peoples are preserved in the southeastern coastal zone, in particular the areas of Guangdong, Fujian and Zhejiang. Interestingly enough, these populations—such as the Tanka, Hakka, and Cantonese—are today, without question, considered Han, but those groups such as the Zhuang of Guangxi Province, who are remarkably similar to their Han neighbors of the north, are not regarded by anyone in China as Han.

As to what is Han, that's a difficult question. Extensive ethnic mixing took place from the third to the sixth century as waves of Huns and Xianbi tribes from the north swept through the heartland of China, along the banks of the Yellow River, where the Han population was concentrated. At the same time, groups of Han Chinese migrated in large numbers southward, forcing out, absorbing or living separately alongside the ethnic peoples they encountered, such as the Miao and Zhuang. Indeed, after centuries of interracial mixing, the gigantic Han "race" is characterized by a broad range of cultural and physical differences.

There has been both success and failure in the assimilation of non-Han peoples. In some cases, the process has not been easy or peaceful, as observed in Tibet. Historically, the Tibetan population had accepted Qing dynasty rule until the downfall of the dynasty in 1911, thereafter achieving a certain degree of autonomy. Proud and self-reliant, Tibetans were not willing to accept the Han-dominated Chinese government's claim to the territory. Tibetan resistance to Han occupation in some areas lasted through the 1950s, and opposition has been revived in recent years.

In other cases, assimilation has been thorough and swift. The Manchu (who were Jurched people living as hunters and herdsmen) entered China in the 17th century and founded the Qing dynasty. Initially, they held on to their language and culture, but eventually they adapted completely to Han culture, manners, and ways of life, and by the end of the Qing, even the last emperor, Puyi, could speak little, if any, of his native culture's mother tongue.

Today, the Chinese government is striving to improve the standard of living for the minority races while officially respecting the unique customs and traditions of each group. For example, use of a minority's spoken and written language is accepted, there is greater economic independence than in non-autonomous regions, vast improvements have been made in the field of education, and traditional forms of music, dance and drama are enthusiastically supported. China's official policy on minorities is far more sensitive to minority issues than that of many other nations, although assimilation of minorities is the ultimate goal. Of course this policy has been violated and poorly implemented in some instances, and it is not easy to balance the preservation of ethnic identity with the urgency of modernization. The task is troublesome and delicate, with no simple answers.

But one of the best ways a nation's identity can be relished and remembered alongside the homogenizing effects of developing industries and technology is through the continuing performance of festivals. Within China, each ethnic group has a distinct way of life and unique style of celebration, from the Miao of Guizhou Province in the south who dance to copper drums to the Mongolian horsemen of northern China who race each other across endless grasslands. Their celebrations excite the senses, with festival components reflecting the primary elements of life—earth, wind, water and fire. As many festival watchers will agree, the most immediate and vital elements of celebration are directly linked to the elements that surround and sustain life, helping to create a special mood and atmosphere for events that will long be remembered in the minds of the participants.

Altogether, China's more than 90 million minority people add a fascinating chapter to the annals of festival lore and holiday ritual. From the Achang to the Zhuang, their independent spirit and cultural identity show a diversity unknown to many Westerners, who still harbor stereotypes of a homogenized China.

FESTIVALS OF EARTH

The Nadam Fair (Mongolian)

Across wide open plains, the Mongols of northern China (numbering well over two million) ride the land, as they have for centuries, galloping over limitless horizons herding camels, cattle, sheep, and yaks. Led first by the powerful armies of Genghis Khan and later by Genghis' grandson, Kublai, in the 13th century, the Mongols became the first non-Han to rule the whole of China. Along with Turks, Tunguses and others, the Mongols numbered over a million. Today, most Chinese Mongols live in Inner Mongolia, but they have also settled as far into China's interior as Henan Province.

Their festivals celebrate the conquest of land through skillful contests of wrestling, horse racing, and archery. During the Nadam Fair held in the seventh lunar month, champion wrestlers grapple and horsemen vie with one another in arduous races covering miles of grassland. Centuries ago Nadam (the Mongol word for recreation) took place during ceremonies of political import, at religious events honoring the teachings of Lamaism (a special form of Buddhism which developed in Tibet where indigenous Tibetan beliefs [Bon] intermingled with the teachings of Buddhist saints and sages), or when specialized rites were made at sacred stone landmarks and outdoor altars. Today, Nadam is widely appreciated as a sporting festival, arts fair, and national holiday.

Id Corban and Lesser Bairam

Along the pastures and plains, the valleys and oases of China's steppelands live the Turkic Uygurs, Kazaks, Uzbeks, Tartars, and Hui.

These are the most numerous of the 16 minorities that inhabit the regions surrounding the branches of one of the world's oldest thoroughfares, the Silk Route. The Silk Route within China originated at Dunhuang and progressed northwest through the Gansu Corridor where it divided into two branches, northern and southern routes which passed along the rims of the arid and dangerous Tarim Basin. The routes joined at Kashgar and then continued over the mountains north into Tashkent and Samarkand or south into Bactria. This was the ancient trade route linking China to Rome that was crossed by traveler and storyteller Marco Polo, who gave the West its most detailed description of 13th-century China.

The minorities living in the provinces of Xinjiang, Ningxia, Gansu, and Qinghai are mostly Muslims, celebrating many of the same festivals observed by Muslims in the Middle East. Two of their most important holidays are religious events: the Id Corban (Festival of Sacrifice), celebrated on the 10th day of the 12th month in the Islamic calendar and the Lesser Bairam (the Festival of Fast-Breaking), which begins on the first of the 10th month.

Id Corban, also called the Day of Grand Prayer, is a time when the animals of the land are sacrificed as offerings (in honor of the prophet Abraham's near-sacrifice of his son Isaac). Hymns are chanted and friends and relatives gather together for joyous reunions with singing, dancing, and feasting on this day. Kazak horsemen celebrate the festival with tournaments showing their equestrian prowess, such as snatching sheep off the ground while on horseback, or through courting games where girls chase after boys in flirtatious riding parties.[See color plate 12b.]

The Lesser Bairam celebrates the end of the fast of Ramadan, which commemorates the first revelation of the *Koran,* the sacred book of Islam. At dawn, followers of Islam pray in mosques and then begin a lively day of greeting friends and consuming delicious snacks of milk, tea, dried peaches, apricots, raisins, honey, and deep-fried sesame cakes. In the streets of Kashgar in west Xinjiang, men wearing embroidered skull caps, women in veils, and excited children

A young Uygur maiden garbed in her festive best (Xinjiang, China).

dressed in their festive best watch dancers twirling and stomping, and musicians playing drums, tambourines and lutes. Everyone gives thanks to Allah for all they have received and then asks for blessings for the future ahead. [See color plates 10a, b.]

The Danu Festival (Yao)

In the labyrinthine valleys of Guangxi, the Yao people, who number over one million, celebrate the fruits of the land during the New Year Festival on the first day of the first lunar month. A more spectacular event, however, is the Danu Festival which occurs once every few years on the 29th day of the fifth lunar month. The highlight of the occasion is the copper drum dance performed with hollow, bottomless copper cylinders. Women dance to the rhythmic beat of the drums—one drum being played off against another in musical competitions rated by audience applause and numerous toasts to the best performers. As legend has it, the celebration is in honor of the Yao goddess Miluoto, whose youngest daughter was responsible for bountiful harvests. She prevented birds and animals from devastating her crops by driving the creatures away with the sounds of the copper drums she played outside in the fields.

Munaozongge Gathering (Jingpo)

The Jingpo tribespeople in the mountain valleys of Yunnan also celebrate the harvest with dancing and singing on a festive occasion known as *Munaozongge*. Parading to wooden drums and gongs accompanied by the high-pitched *dongba* (something like an oxhorn), men and women step to the music hand in hand. The leader of the performance wears a striking headdress of peacock feathers, a symbol of beauty, fortune, and dignity. Her graceful motions recall the ancient legend of the peacock's dazzling performance in front of the first ancestors of the Jingpo people. [See color plate 12a.]

Dashing contrasts and stark geometry of the Yao costume.

FESTIVALS OF WATER

Water Splashing Festival (Dai)

As a symbol of purification, fecundity, and regeneration, water plays a central role in this major New Year celebration of the over 600,000 Dai people of Yunnan Province. On the second day of the festival, which is celebrated between the 24th and 26th of the *sixth* month instead of the common date, people splash water on each other as a way of bestowing blessings—the greater the soaking, the more happiness for the recipient. [See color plate 11.]

The day of water splashing is an especially festive time for the Dai who live in southern Yunnan, near Laos and Burma, one of China's most sparsely settled areas—an up-and-down land that suffers periodically from drought, monsoons, and harsh climatic change. They take full advantage of the festival to symbolically send off the old and bring in the new. The first day is celebrated with dragon boat races, each village being represented by a boat with a carved wooden dragon's head at the bow. By evening, villages gather together to sing and dance to the rhythm of drums, flutes, and gongs. Peacocks thrive in the land known as "South of the Yun Mountains" and native folk dances are performed in imitation of this splendid bird. Firecrackers—usually bamboo tubes filled with gunpowder and then fired off—burst into the night air.

As is the case with many community celebrations, festivals are also a time when girls and boys are encouraged to socialize through games and dance. On the third day there is an event called "throwing pouches" *(diubao)* where girls and boys line up and toss colorful cloth sacks to one another. A miss is acknowledged by giving flowers to the tosser. This coquettish game of throw and catch gives young people an opportunity to openly pay attention to one another and engenders a possible romantic interest for the year ahead.

Two young women of Tu nationality from Qinghai.

The Bathing Festival (Tibetan)

Roaming the rugged snow-clad mountains of western China and the provinces of Qinghai, Sichuan, Gansu, and Yunnan are the tenacious Tibetans who survive the rigors of their environment by drinking ample servings of hot tea and yak butter. Their religious foundation, like the Mongolians, is Lamaism, the religion of the lamas or "superior ones." In Lhasa, Tibet's capital, beneath the splendor of the Potala Palace, one can hear prayer wheels spinning and people chanting *om mani padme hum* ("Hail to the Jewel in the Lotus"), an invocation to the Bodhisattva.

One of the most festive times of the year is early autumn when Tibetans celebrate an annual outdoor bathing rite by the Lhasa River. The pure, clear autumn water is valued for its restorative powers, and because the temperature of the river is seasonally warm, people of all ages can enjoy a revitalizing splash in the river. According to legend, this custom is over eight hundred years old and was based on the blessings received from Guanyin, the Buddhist Goddess of Mercy, who alleviated a life-threatening epidemic by pouring holy water from her jade vase into the lakes, rivers, and ponds of Tibet. People who bathed in the waters were cured and subsequently led a life of good health and general prosperity. Such is the hope every year for the autumn bathers of the Lhasa River.

Third Moon Fair (Bai)

Yunnan Province is home to the Bai people, who number more than one million in population. One of their main festival attractions is the Third Moon Fair when a number of ethnic groups—Yi, Tibetan, Hui, Lisu, Naxi, and Han—gather together for a week of trading and cultural exchange.

Legend attributes the origin of this event (which takes place between the 15th and 20th of the third month) to a marriage between two people of the water—a fisherman and the princess of the dragon king of Lake Er Hai. Every year, on the 15th of the third moon, a fair was held, where gods and goddesses admired precious gems, rare treasures and medicinal herbs. One year, the princess took the fisherman to the fair, and after returning to earth they told the villagers of the holiday, which inspired people to start a county fair of their own.

Held the same time as the fair of the gods, the event featured a panoply of local attractions from silk threads and pearl necklaces to felt hats and butter pots to farm implements and fish nets. A centuries-old tradition reaching back to the Tang dynasty, the Third Month Fair is in many respects as much a festival as a bazaar, with horse racing, ball and chess games, dancing and archery contests all adding to the gala nature of the occasion.

FESTIVALS OF THE WIND

Catching-the-Autumn Festival (Miao)

Sailing through the wind in a high-flying swing is at the heart of the Miao people's Catching-the-Autumn Festival as celebrated in Hunan Province. A delightful Cinderella legend provides one explanation of the origin of this custom. In ancient times lived a handsome young Miao hunter. One day he shot down an eagle and discovered a delicate embroidered shoe caught in its talons. Determined to find its owner, the man built a swing in which the girls in the village could sit and try on the slipper. Eventually, he found the shoe's owner, a lovely young maiden who was virtuous and kindhearted. As the legend goes, they married, and lived happily ever after. To this day the swing remains an integral part of the harvest-day celebration for welcoming home the village hunters and finding someone to capture your heart.

In some areas of Yunnan the swing takes on larger, symbolic dimensions as part of an elaborate annual ceremony in which the village priest, tightly grasping the long vine of the swing, launches out over the village. For an instant he sees the entire community—everyone is in festive outfits, their homes are in good repair, and the rice on the mountainside is ready to be harvested. Giving thanks to the ancestors, he swings back down and steps off, returning once more to the level of the watching crowd. [See color plates 10 a, b.]

There are at least five million Miao in China living in Guizhou, Hunan, Yunnan, Guangxi, Sichuan, and Guangdong, with subgroups extending beyond China's borders into Laos, Vietnam, and Thailand. The

Miao are noted for their beautifully embroidered aprons, turbans and collars, and priceless heirlooms of silver. It is in fact through traditional costumes that the Miao distinguish their five major subdivisions: the Black, Red, White, Blue, and Flowery Miao. Strong in self-reliance and born to the limitless expanses of the mountains, the Miao have maintained a vigorous spirit of independence and cultural integrity through centuries of difficult struggles.

March the Third Festival (Zhuang)

Carried through the air in a celebration of springtime are the unique songfests of the Zhuang people. The Zhuang are the largest of the national minorities of China with over 13 million people living in in Guangxi Province. Young men and women celebrate their tradition of song and dance in groves of bamboo or on grassy slopes by singing songs of love and romance to each other through a method of vocalization called dialog singing. Although the Zhuang are difficult to distinguish physically from their Han neighbors, they hold tightly to their own festival traditions with thousands of participants singing together on this day of welcoming in the spring.

FESTIVALS OF FIRE

Festival of Torches (Yi)

Regarded through the ages as the divine agent of warmth and transformation, fire is at the center of the Yi people's spectacular Festival of Torches. Well over four million in number, the Yi live in the provinces of Yunnan, Sichuan, and Guizhou.

Legend claims the festival originated during a period when bamboo torches were ignited to kill swarms of locusts that were destroying mountain crops. To commemorate the successful harvest, every year on the 24th of the sixth lunar month people dance in the evening with lit torches, "splashing fire" on friends that they meet along the way. The celebrants sprinkle an inflammable resin mix over their torches, causing cascades of sparks to shower down on the passersby. Throughout the evening, and for two more days, men dressed in black turbans and women with colorful skirts of red, yellow, and black, stroll down the street to observe the festival events—sheep fights, archery, and horse racing—and to cheer on the contestants of these games.

The Rocket Festival (Dong)

The Dong hill tribes, spread throughout the provinces of Guizhou, Hunan, and Guangxi, celebrate the ear-splitting, eye-dazzling Rocket Festival. This event takes place at various times throughout the year, the date differing from region to region.

Started in the Qing dynasty, this celebration was originally conceived of as a way of promoting selected marketplaces through attracting participants with a brilliant display of exploding fireworks and shooting rockets. As practiced today, the rockets are filled with gunpowder and contain a small ring that is released when the rocket is fired into the sky. To the sound of drums, gongs, and *suonas* (a Chinese-style oboe), the ground is then quickly scoured by eager young men who hope to find the fallen ring, a coveted symbol of good fortune for the year ahead. The bangs and crackles of fireworks are as essential as anywhere in China, startling away bad tidings and bursting out with hope for the future.

Sword-Ladder Festival (Lisu)

Firewalking is the featured event in the Sword Ladder Festival of the 500,000 Lisu living in Yunnan Province. Walking on live coals while juggling burning embers, several men chosen from each community exercise supreme self control in shamanistic purification ceremonies.

The New Year is another occasion for the Lisu to use fire to drive away evil influences. At this time, the Lisu in Thailand (who migrated there from Burma at the turn of the century) watch the senior shamans of their villages go into trance. While in this elevated state, they blow fireballs of flaming lard to nullify any bad forces. In addition to the priests' specialized rituals, the New Year schedule of events includes the ceremonial planting of trees, special offerings of rice cakes and pork to village gods and leaders, and folk dancing to the accompaniment of pipes and lutes. The women make an especially stunning appearance at the festivities dressed in their New Year finery of elegantly embroidered tunics and turbans accented by massive amounts of silver jewelry.

The gala affair continues through evening and lasts until dawn, when the head priests announce that the events have come to an end as the blazing sun heralds a new day and the beginning of another new year.

CHINA'S FIFTY-FIVE NATIONAL MINORITIES

Over one million in population:

NATIONALITY	AREA
Zhuang	Guangxi, Yunnan, Guangdong
Hui	Ningxia, Gansu
Uygur	Xinjiang
Yi	Sichuan, Yunnan, Guizhou, Guangxi, Gansu
Miao	Guizhou, Hunan, Yunnan, Guangxi, Sichuan
Manchu	Lioaning, Jilin, Heilongjiang, Hebei, Beijing, Inner Mongolia
Tibetan	Tibet, Qinghai, Sichuan, Gansu, Yunnan
Tujia	Hunan, Hubei
Mongol	Inner Mongolia, Xinjiang, Liaoning
Bouyei	Guizhou
Korean	Jilin, Heilongjiang, Inner Mongolia
Dong	Guizhou, Hunan, Guangxi
Yao	Guangxi, Hunan, Yunnan, Guangdong, Guizhou
Bai	Yunnan
Hani	Yunnan

100,000 to one million:

Kazak	Xinjiang, Gansu, Qinghai
Dai	Yunnan
Li	Guangdong
Lisu	Yunnan, Sichuan
Lahu	Yunnan
Wa	Yunnan
Shui	Jiangxi, Guangdong, Guizhou, Guangxi
NATIONALITY	**AREA**
Dongxiang	Gansu, Xinjiang
Naxi	Yunnan, Sichuan
Tu	Qinghai, Gansu
Kirghir	Xinjiang, Heilongjiang
Quang	Sichuan

10,000 to 100,000:

Daur	Inner Mongolia, Heilongjiang, Xinjiang
Jingpo	Yunnan
Mulao	Guangxi
Xibo	Xinjiang, Liaoning, Jilin
Sala	Qinghai, Gansu
Bulang	Yunnan
Gelao	Guizhou, Gunagxi, Sichuan, Hunan
Maonan	Guangxi
She	Fujian, Zhejiang
Tajik	Xinjiang
Pumi	Yunnan
Nu	Yunnan

10,000 to 100,000, continued:

Achang	Yunnan
Ewenki	Inner Mongolia, Heilongjiang
Uzbek	Xinjiang
Benglong	Yunnan
Jing	Guangxi
Jinuo	Guangxi
Yugur	Gansu

NATIONALITY	**AREA**

Under 10,000:

Baoan	Gansu
Menba	Tibet
Dulong	Yunnan
Oroqen	Inner Mongolia, Heilongjiang
Tartar	Xinjiang
Russian	Xinjiang
Luoba	Tibet
Hezhe	Heilongjiang
Gaoshan	Taiwan, Fujian

APPENDIX

The Chinese Calendar

The traditional Chinese festival calendar is a type of lunar, or more accurately a lunar-solar, calendar.

Lunar time is linked with the regular appearances of the full moon—the moon being the most obvious indicator of change in the sky and thus a natural marker for human events. The lunar calendar is made up of 12 lunar months of 29 or 30 days each.

However, because the position of the sun at the solstice and equinox determines the seasons, any agricultural civilization must follow solar time (the sun makes things grow, not the moon). The solar year, with its four seasons, is 365 days long and is divided into 24 15-day periods known collectively as the 24 Joints or Breaths.

This set of 24 periods almost always starts on February 5 with *Lichun,* meaning "Spring Begins." Only two of China's major festivals are based on the solar calendar—Qingming and the Winter Solstice—all others are dated by the lunar calendar.

Anyone who studies and uses such a lunar-solar calendar, however, faces a major problem—how to reconcile the solar year (approximately 365 days) with the lunar cycle (given that one lunar month equals approximately 29 and one-half days, making a 354-day year). There is also the problem of accounting for partial days or months in the calendar. The common solar calendar accounts for partial days by inserting an "interca-

lary day" every four years (February 29). The Chinese lunar calendar accounts for partial months by inserting an "intercalary" or leap month, usually at three-year but sometimes at two-year intervals.

The official calendar also indicated other kinds of time. From very early times the hours, days, months and years were marked by a system of counting based on one cycle of 10 counting signs called the "Heavenly Stems" *(tiangan)* and another cycle of 12 counting signs called the "Earthly Branches" *(dizhi)*.

The 24 Solar Terms

PINYIN	CHARACTER	ENGLISH	GREGORIAN CALENDAR DATE
Lichun	立春	Spring Begins	February 5
Yushui	雨水	The Rains	February 19
Jingzhe	驚蟄	Insects Awaken	March 5
Chunfen	春分	Spring Equinox	March 20
Qingming	清明	Clear and Bright	April 5
Guyu	谷雨	Grain Rain	April 20
Lixia	立夏	Summer Begins	May 5
Xiaoman	小滿	Grain Fills Out	May 21
Mangzhong	芒種	Grain in Ear	June 2
Xiazhi	夏至	Summer Solstice	June 21
Xiaoshu	小暑	Small Heat	July 7
Dashu	大暑	Great Heat	July 23
Liqiu	立秋	Autumn Begins	August 7
Chushu	処暑	Limit of Heat	August 23

PINYIN	CHARACTER	ENGLISH	GREGORIAN CALENDAR DATE
Bailu	白露	White Dew	September 8
Qiufen	秋分	Autumn Equinox	September 23
Hanlu	寒露	Cold Dew	October 8
Shuangjiang	霜降	Frost Descends	October 23
Lidong	立冬	Winter Begins	November 7
Xiaoxue	小雪	Small Snow	November 22
Daxue	大雪	Great Snow	December 7
Dongzhi	冬至	Winter Solstice	December 21
Xiaohan	小寒	Small Cold	January 6
Dahan	大寒	Great Cold	January 26

The 10 Heavenly Stems in sequence are:

jia 甲 , yi 乙 , bing 丙 , ding 丁 , wu 戊 ,
ji 己 , geng 庚 , xin 辛 , ren 壬 , gui 癸 .

The 12 Earthly Branches in sequence are:

zi 子 , chou 丑 , yin 寅 , mao 卯 , chen 辰 ,
si 巳 , wu 午 , wei 未 , shen 申 , you 酉 ,
xu 戌 , hai 亥 .

When the Stems and Branches are combined (only odd numbers can be associated with odd numbers, and evens with evens), a list of 60 pairs is produced. Each calendar year corresponds to one of these pairs of two cyclical counting signs—the first being one of the 10 Heavenly Stems and the second being one of the 12 Earthly Branches. For example, designating the calendar year 1984 combines the first Heavenly Stem *jia* with the first Earthly Branch *zi* to form the unit *jiazi,* which happens to be the beginning of the current 60 year cycle (the cycle will repeat again in the year 2044).

The 12 Earthly Branches are simple enough to identify because they correspond, one by one, to the twelve animals of the Chinese zodiac in the following sequence: *zi* with rat, *chou* with ox, *yin* with tiger, *mao* with rabbit, *chen* with dragon, *si* with snake, *wu* with horse, *wei* with ram, *shen* with monkey, *you* with rooster, *xu* with dog, and *hai* with pig.

Each of the 10 Heavenly Stems correspond, two by two, to the Five Colors in the following sequence: *jia* and *yi* with azure; *bing* and *ding* with red; *wu* and *ji* with yellow; *geng* and *xin* with white, and *ren* and *gui* with black.

Thus, we can also describe a year according to its color-animal combination. The calendar year 1984 would, for example, be described as the Year of the Azure Rat, 1985 *(yichou)* is the Year of the Azure Ox, and so on.

Major Birthdays and Festivals

Lunar Calendar

First Moon

DAY 1   New Year's Day.

DAY 9   Birthday of the Jade Emperor, supreme deity of the pantheon of Chinese gods.

DAY 15   The Lantern Festival.

Second Moon

DAY 2   Birthday of the Lord of the Earth, Tudigong, who is depicted as an old gentleman with a long flowing beard, and who resides on every street or neighborhood to keep the peace and ensure general prosperity.

DAY 3   Birthday of the God of Literature, Wenchang, who is usually represented holding a pen and book on which is written the phrase "Heaven determines literary achievement."

DAY 15   Birthday of Lao Tze (Laozi) (b. ca. 604 B.C.), founder of Taoism, reputed to have written the *Tao Te Ching (Daode Jing)* (Classic of the Way and Its Power), a combination of poetry, mysticism and philosophical speculation that promotes non-interference as a way of life. Priests and hermits studied the Tao (literally, "The Way") in hope of attaining immortality and supernatural powers.

DAY 19   Birthday of Guanyin (One Who Hears Sounds/Prayers), the Buddhist Goddess of Mercy, who is honored as a protective guardian of women and children.

Third Moon

DAY 3   Birthday of Xuantian Shangdi, the Supreme Lord of the Dark Heaven, who presides over the North Pole and is worshiped as a controller of floods and rains. He is the presiding deity of many exotic cults.

Third Moon, continued

DAY 23   Birthday of the Queen of Heaven, Tian Hou, popularly known as Mazu, Goddess of the Sea.

Solar Calendar
Qing Ming, the Clear Brightness Festival *(usually April 4 or 5)*

Fourth Moon

DAY 8   Birthday of Sakyamuni Buddha, founder of Buddhism, whose teachings on the release from suffering through meditation and the search for enlightenment spread through China beginning in the first century A.D. For lay followers, Buddhism generally provides a means of dealing with life after death through rewards for good deeds in heaven and punishment for evil in hell.

DAY 14   Birthday of Lu Dongbin, the most prominent of the legendary Eight Immortals and an eccentric Taoist adept who aids the downtrodden and protects barbers and pharmacists.

DAY 18   Birthday of Huato, patron god of medicine.

Fifth Moon

DAY 5   Dragon Boat Festival.

Sixth Moon

DAY 13   Birthday of Lu Ban, patron deity of builders and carpenters.

DAY 24   Birthday of Guan Di, God of Martial Activities, a historical figure of great military prowess who lived in the third century A.D. and assisted Liu Bei in his efforts to unify China. Patron deity of merchants and judges and those who engage in contracts. Presides over many exorcistic cults.

Seventh Moon

DAY 7   Meeting Day of the Weaving Maiden and Herdboy.

DAY 15   Hungry Ghost Festival.

DAY 30   Birthday of Dizang Wang, king of the netherworld, who opens the gates of hell and rescues suffering souls.

Eighth Moon

DAY 15   Mid-Autumn Festival.

DAY 16   Birthday of Sun Wukong, the Monkey King, Great Sage Equal to Heaven. Popularized in the novel *Journey to the West,* the mischievous Monkey King assisted the saintly monk Xuan Zang on his journey to India to obtain sacred Buddhist texts. To this day Monkey is widely celebrated as a trickster figure of immeasurable talent and cunning wit.

DAY 27   Birthday of Confucius (Kong Fuzi) (551–479 B.C.), China's greatest sage, whose teachings about good government and harmonious relations have molded Chinese civilization and philosophical thought for generations. In Taiwan, the official date of Confucius' birthday is fixed at September 28.

Ninth Moon

DAY 9   Double Ninth Day.

Tenth Moon

DAY 1   Sending Off the Winter Clothes.

DAY 5   Birthday of Bodhidharma, the founding patriarch of Chan Buddhism (Zen in Japan). Chan teaches that reality is empty, or void, and can't be expressed with words or thought, but only understood by intuition, completely and instantly.

Eleventh Moon

DAY 17   Birthday of Amitabha Buddha, meaning Infinite Light, who presides over the Pure Land, a fertile western paradise filled with flowers, jewels, and fragrant waters where those fortunate enough to arrive there can hear the truth of Buddhism and attain enlightenment.

Twelfth Moon

DAY 8   Celebration of Sakyamuni achieving enlightenment.

DAY 23   Kitchen God reports to the Jade Emperor.

Symbols of Celebration— A Supplementary Glossary

The sweet fragrance of incense, the power of charms, the explosion of firecrackers and an abundance of cakes and pastries—these are some of the essential symbols of celebration that transform an ordinary day into something special.

To give the reader an introduction to the standard inventory of items necessary for a festival as well as an idea of the rich nomenclature of the Chinese language, the following lists of firecrackers, longevity noodles, deity incense, spirit money, etc. are provided below:

Firecrackers

Flags of fire	*qihuo*	旗火
Golden plates	*jinpan*	金盤
Double kicking feet	*ertijiao*	二踢脚
Ten explosions flying to heaven	*feitianshixiang*	飛天十嚮
Peonies strung on a thread	*xianchuanmudan*	線穿牡丹
Flower pots	*huapen*	花盆
Fire trees	*huoshu*	火樹
Lanterns of heaven and earth	*tiandideng*	天地燈
Eight-cornered rockets	*bajiaozi*	八角子
Five devils noisily splitting apart	*wuguinaopan*	五鬼鬧判

These were selected from ANNUAL FESTIVALS IN PEKING (translated by Derk Bodde).

Foods

Longevity noodles   壽麵   *shoumian.* At birthday celebrations, extra long noodles are eaten, with great care being taken not to bite them off short as this might reduce the longevity of the person whose birthday is being honored.

Goodness peaches   善桃   *shantao.* Rice or wheat flour cakes made in the shape of peaches to symbolize long life.

Paired tortoises   雙連龜   *shuangliangui.* Shaped like a figure eight and filled with red bean paste, these wheat flour buns represent happiness and are used on the birthdays of deities or people.

Wealth cakes   發糕   *fagao.* White steamed sponge cake with the top split open to form a cross. The split grows larger as the cake is baked and rises, symbolizing the auspicious wish of "becoming wealthy."

Mountain flavors and sea tastes   山珍海味
shanzhenhaiwei. Four condiments used in Taiwanese cooking—fresh ginger, granulated sugar, salt and red beans—that are also placed in dishes as food offerings for gods and ancestors.

Stacks of pink-colored "goodness" peaches symbolizing longevity.

Incense

Pure incense   淨香   *jingxiang* (powdered sandalwood)

Small incense   小香   *xiaoxiang*

Amba incense   唵叭香 *ambaxiang* (extra long, thick incense sticks)

Ritual incense   禮香   *lixiang* (large flat incense stick made from pasting and tying four incense sticks together)

Bundled kindling 束柴 *shuchai* (sandalwood chips)

Incense fire   香火   *xianghuo.* Small red pouch or medallion filled with incense ashes from a temple urn (or folded paper charm) to be worn around the neck or hung in one's auto.

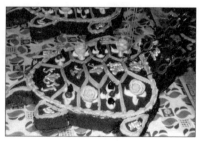

A tortoise cake with chocolate frosting.

Varieties of incense.

Spirit Money

Buddha hair and Buddha plumes 佛毛（羽）*fomao (yu)*. Used to worship one's ancestors, these thin yellow sheets of paper are inscribed with incantations and prayers and then burned to help departed spirits enter the Pure Land (Western Paradise).

Deity clothing 神衣 *shenyi*. These thin yellow sheets decorated with silver foil, gold wash, dragons, and longevity characters are folded in half and wrapped around packets of spirit money which are burned as offerings to the gods on festival days.

Longevity gold 壽金 *shoujin*. The basic currency of the spirit world is a sheet of yellow paper brushed with gold wash and decorated with a picture of the gods of Happiness, Wealth and Longevity. It is usually packaged in thick bundles and offered by burning to the major deities.

Armor and horses 甲馬 *jiama*. Images of armor and horses are stamped on white paper that is bundled together in thick packets and offered to a deity's assistants and guardian soldiers. The money packets are burned in a ritual to reward the soldiers."

(This list selected and adapted from Alvin P. Cohen's, "Fiscal Remarks on Some Folk Religion Temples in Taiwan," MONUMENTA SERICA (32) 1976: 85–158.)

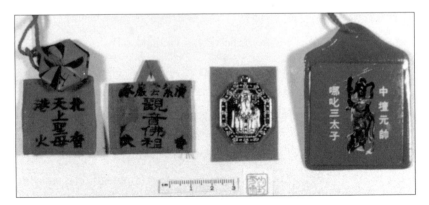

Red pouches containing incense ashes.

SETTING A TABLE FIT FOR THE GODS

Foods are used in the religious aspects of festivals as a way of communicating with gods, ghosts, and ancestors. Once the spirits consume the "essence" of the food, it is shared with friends and relatives. The arrangements and types of food will vary according to region, occasion, and festival, but the following are some general guidelines on the hierarchical ranking of food for events ranging from an ordinary act of reverence to an ancestral offering dinner to a god's birthday celebration—the complexity depending on the importance of the event and the magnitude of the favor requested of the gods.

Simple *Bai* ("Worshiping") Rite

Level one: three small sticks of incense.

Level two: additional offerings of tea and fruit such as jujubes, oranges, tangerines, muskmelon, mango, pear, star-fruit, papaya or pineapple. Some temples prepare plates arranged with four different kinds of fruit *(siguo)*. Different kinds of sweet preserved fruits arranged in four large cups are called "four colors" *(sise)*.

Offerings are also arranged in patterns of ones, threes and fives.

Common *Bai* Rite

To the simple rite is added beverages of wine and tea, a bowl of noodles, or some basic staple food and fruit.

Important *Bai* Rite

Basic meat dishes are added to the common rite. The most typical dishes are the three sacrificial meats *(sansheng)* which include fish, pork, and chicken (or duck and goose) with pork in the center as the main dish.

Highest *Bai* Rite

This features a whole pig (which is usually presented roasted in South China). The five sacrificial meats *(wusheng)* —pork, rabbit, chicken, duck, and fish—are arranged for important occasions along with piles of red steamed buns and red-colored eggs for special favors. (Alternatives to the sacrificial meats are vegetarian sacrificial foods *[caishengli]* made of dough and formed into the shape of chickens, pigs, etc.)

Offering of a roasted pig with a pineapple in its mouth.

(This list adapted from E. N. Anderson, Jr., and Marja L. Anderson's "Modern China: South" in FOOD IN CHINESE CULTURE.)

Symbols and Images of Long Life,

Happiness and Good Fortune: A Pictorial Glossary

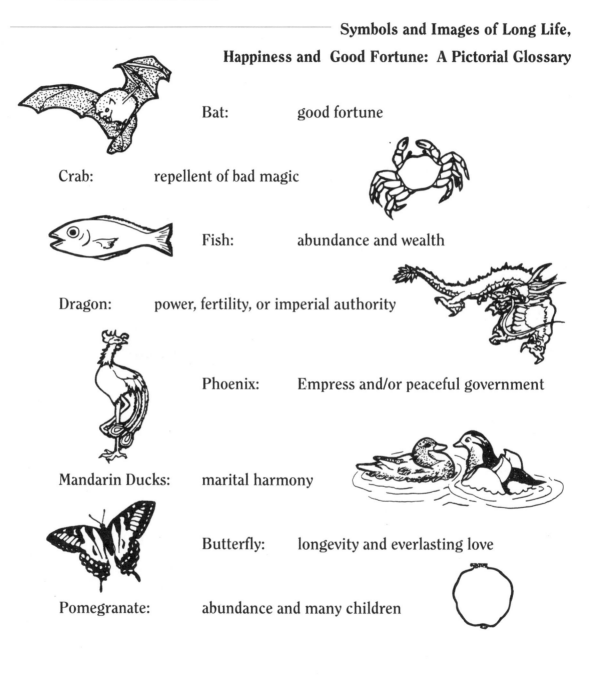

Bat: good fortune

Crab: repellent of bad magic

Fish: abundance and wealth

Dragon: power, fertility, or imperial authority

Phoenix: Empress and/or peaceful government

Mandarin Ducks: marital harmony

Butterfly: longevity and everlasting love

Pomegranate: abundance and many children

Clouds: good fortune and happiness

Lotus: purity

Tiger: courage and bravery

Chrysanthemum: long life

Bottle-Gourd: a magical container

Crane   longevity:

Frog: wealth and protection

Pine Tree: longevity and endurance

Peach: immortality

Tortoise: permanence

CHARACTER GLOSSARY OF SELECTED CHINESE WORDS AND NAMES

Ba Ye	八爺	fengshui	風水	hunge	婚歌
baishen	拜神	fengshuideng	風水燈	jian	尖
baizitu	百子圖	fengzheng	風箏	jiangbaxian	降八仙
bao	暴	foshou	佛手	jiaozi	餃子
bazi	八字	fu	福	Jie Zitui	介子推
bu bu deng gao	步步登高	gengzhitu	耕織圖	kuge	哭歌
caishengli	菜牲禮	guanxiamo	觀蝦蟆	labazhou	臘八粥
chahua	茶花	Guanyin	觀音	Li Sao	離騷
Chang E	嫦娥	gui	鬼	lichun	立春
chongyangjie	重陽節	hanchuan	旱船	lilao	醴酪
chunjie	春節	haoxiongdi	好兄弟	lohuayuan	落花園
chunlian	春聯	He He Erxian	和合二仙	lu	祿
dachun	打春	henian quanhe	賀年全盒	lushi	律詩
danu	達努	hongbao	紅包	Mang Shen	芒神
dengjie	燈節	Hou Yi	后羿	mazhang	馬張
diubao	丟包	Huan Jing	桓景	Mazu	媽祖
dizhi	地支	huapaohui	花炮會	menshen	門神
dongba	洞巴	huiqi	晦氣	Mulian	目蓮
duanwujie	端午節	hun	魂	munaozongge	目腦縱歌
Fei Changfang	費長房	yinjian	陰間	nian	年

niangao	年糕	sise	四色	yuanxiao	元宵
nianhua	年畫	suona	哨吶	yuanxiaojie	元宵節
pingan	平安	tangyuan	湯圓	Yuchi Jingde	尉遲敬德
pudu	普渡	taozi	桃子	yuebing	月餅
Qi Ye	七爺	tiangan	天干	yueguang ma'er	月光馬兒
qianchang	千張	Tianhou	天后	Yuexialaoye	月下老爺
qiangyen	搶宴	tiegeng haitang	貼梗海棠	Yuhuangdi	五皇帝
Qianliyen	千里眼	Tu'er Ye	兔兒爺	yulanhui	盂蘭會
Qin Qiong	秦瓊	Tudi gong	土地公	yulanpen	盂蘭盆
Qingming	清明	wannianqing	萬年青	Yulu	鬱壘
Qingti	清提	wansui	萬歲	Zao Jun	竈君
qixijie	七夕爺	weilu	圍爐	zheng	箏
Qu Yuan	屈原	Wu Gang	吳剛	Zhongkui	鍾旭
que chuan	怯船	wudu	五毒	zhongqiujie	中秋節
renao	熱鬧	wusheng	五牲	zhongyuan	中元
sansheng	三牲	xi	喜	zongzi	粽子
shangtiantang	上天堂	xiaonian	小年		
shanlaoshi	山老師	yang	陽		
Shentu	神荼	yangge	秧歌		
shuilaoye	水老爺	yasuiqian	壓歲錢		
shuixianhua	水仙花	yijia zhizhu	一家之主		
Shunfenger	順風耳	yin	陰		
siguo	四果	yuanbao	元寶		

Chronology of Dynasties

Xia	21st–16th century B.C.
Shang	16th–11th century B.C.
Zhou	11th century–256 B.C.
Spring and Autumn	770–476 B.C.
Warring States	475–221 B.C.
Qin	221–206 B.C.
Han	206 B.C.–A.D. 220
Three Kingdoms	220–265
Jin	265–420
Southern and Northern	420–581
Sui	581–618
Tang	618–907
Five Dynasties	907–960
Northern Song	960–1127
Southern Song	1127–1279
Yuan	1279–1368
Ming	1368–1644
Qing	1644–1911
Republican	1912–1949
People's Republic of China	1949–

Notes

Introduction

1. Qi Xing, *Gufeng Minsu,* pp. 121-196.
2. David Faure, "Folk Religion in Hong Kong and the New Territories Today" in *Turning of the Tide,* Julian Pas, ed., pp. 259-270.
3. Julian Pas, "Revival of Temple Worship and Popular Religious Tradition" in *Turning of the Tide,* Julian Pas, ed., pp. 158-185.

New Year Festival

1. Qi Xing, Gufeng Minsu, pp. 103.
2. Arthur Wolf, "Gods, Ghosts and Ancestors" in *Studies in Chinese Society,* Arthur Wolf, ed., pp. 133-135.
3. Alvin Cohen, "A Chinese Temple Keeper Talks About Chinese Folk Religion,"*Asian Folklore Studies* 36 (1977), p.13.
4. Wolfram Eberhard, ed., *Folktales of China,* pp. 194-195.
5. Jiann Hsieh and Ying-hsiung Chou, "Public Aspirations in the New Year Couplets," *Asian Folklore Studies* 40–2 (1981), pp. 130-131.
6. *Ibid,* p. 137.
7. Nancy Zeng Berliner, *Chinese Folk Art,* pp. 202-215.
8. Ellen Laing, "Chinese Peasant Painting: Amateur and Professional," *Art International* 7 (1984), pp. 1-12.
9. Qi Xing, *Gufeng Minsu,* p. 7.
10. Clement Egerton, *The Golden Lotus,* vol. 2, pp. 168-169.
11. Frederick Mote, "Yuan and Ming" in *Food in Chinese Culture,* K. C. Chang, ed., p. 230.
12. *Ibid.,* p. 219.
13. Qi Xing, *Gufeng Minsu,* pp. 20-22.
14. *Ibid.,* pp. 30-33.
15. David Holm, "Folk Art as Propaganda: The *Yangge* Movement in Yan'an" in *Popular Chinese Literature and Performing Arts,* Bonnie McDougall, ed., pp. 16-17.

Dragon Boat Festival

1. Goran Aijmer, *The Dragon Boat Festival on the Hupeh-Hunan Plain, Central China,* passim.
2. Wolfram Eberhard, *Chinese Festivals,* pp. 75-77.

Mid-Autumn Festival

1. Wolfram Eberhard, *Dictionary of Chinese Symbols,* pp. 292-293.
2. Marie-Luise Latsch, *Chinese Traditional Festivals,* pp. 78-80.

Clear Brightness Festival

1. Emily Ahern, *The Cult of the Dead in a Chinese Village,* p. 177.
2. Wolfram Eberhard, *Chinese Festivals,* pp. 118-123.

Feast of the Hungry Ghosts

1. Y. W. Ma and Joseph S. M. Lau, eds., *Traditional Chinese Stories,* p. 452.

Rites of Matrimony

1. Fred Blake, "Death and Abuse in Marriage Laments, *Asian Folklore Studies* 37 (1978), pp. 13-33.
2. David Jordan, "Spirit Brides," *Gods, Ghosts, and Ancestors,* pp. 140-151.

Selected Bibliography

Sources in Chinese

Huang Bocang. *Jieri de chuanshuo* (Legends of Festivals). Changsha: Hunan People's Publishing House,1982.

Qi Xing. *Gufeng minsu* (Ancient Lore and Folk Customs). Hong Kong: Commerical Press, 1987.

Qi Zhiping. *Jieling de gushi* (Stories About Festivals). Taipei: Kongzhong Magazine House, 1980.

Tang Lusun. *Zhongguo chi de gushi* (Stories About Chinese Culinary Traditions). Taipei: Han Guang Cultural Enterprise Co., 1984.

Wang Shizhen. *Zhongguo jieling xisu* (Customs of Chinese Festivals). Hong Kong: Kunlun Publishing House, n.d.

Wu Yingtao. *Taiwan minsu* (Taiwanese Folk Customs). Taipei: Zhong Wen Book Co., 1978.

Wu Youru. *Wushi huapu wubaizhong* (Five Hundred Examples of Wu's Decorative Paintings). Taipei: Wen Hua Book Co., 1975.

Yeqi Chenjin. *Zhongguo jixiang tuan* (Chinese Auspicious Design Patterns). Taipei: Zhong Wen Book Co., 1980.

Sources in English

On Festivals Through the Year

Bredon, Juliet, and Igor Mitrophanow. *The Moon Year, A Record of Chinese Customs and Festivals.* Shanghai: Kelly and Walsh, 1927; reprint, New York: Paragon, 1964; Taipei: Ch'eng Wen Publishing Co. 1972.

Eberhard, Wolfram. *Chinese Festivals.* New York: Henry Shuman, 1952.

Hodous, Lewis. *Folkways in China.* London: Probsthain, 1929.

Jones, Anita. *Chinese Festivals—Feasts—Fortunes.* Taipei: Mei Ya Publications, 1971.

Latsch, Marie-Luise. *Chinese Traditional Festivals.* Beijing: New World Press, 1984.

Law, Joan, and Barbara E. Ward. *Chinese Festivals.* Hong Kong: South China Morning Post, 1982.

Tun Li-ch'en. *Annual Customs and Festivals in Peking.* Translated by Derk Bodde. Hong Kong: Hong Kong University Press, 1965; first edition, Peiping: Henri Vetch, 1936.

On Individual Festivals and Customs

Aijmer, Goran. *The Dragon Boat Festival on the Hupeh-Hunan Plains, Central China.* Ethnographical Museum of Sweden, Monograph Series, no. 9, Stockholm, 1964.

Chao, Wei-pang. "Games at the Mid-Autumn Festival in Kuangtung." *Folklore Studies* 3 (1944): 1–16.

————. "Yang-go, the Rural Theater in Ting-hsien, Hopei." *Folklore Studies* 3 (1944): 17–38.

Holzman, Donald. "The Cold Food Festival in Early Medieval China." *Harvard Journal of Asiatic Studies* 46 (1986): 51–79.

Hsieh, Jiann, and Ying-hsiung Chou. "Public Aspirations in the New Year Couplets: A Comparative Study." *Asian Folklore Studies* 40–2 (1981): 125—149.

Sellmann, James D. "From Myth to Festival: A Structural Analysis of the Chinese New Year Celebration." *Chinese Culture* 23 (1982): 41–58.

Teiser, Stephen F. *The Ghost Festival in Medieval China.* Princeton: Princeton University Press, 1988.

Tirone, Gail. "The Matsu Festival at Peikang, 1986." *Free China Review* 36 (1986): 36–41.

Yang, Ssu-ch'ang. "The Dragon Boat Race in Wu-ling, Hunan." Translated by Chao Wei-pang. *Folklore Studies* 2 (1943): 1–18.

On Religion and Culture

Ahern, Emily. *The Cult of the Dead in a Chinese Village.* Stanford, Calif.: Stanford University Press, 1973.

Bartholomew, Terese Tse. *Myths and Rebuses in Chinese Art.* San Francisco: Asian Art Museum, 1988.

————. *The Hundred Flowers.* San Francisco: Asian Art Museum, 1985.

Berliner, Nancy Zeng. *Chinese Folk Art.* Boston: Little, Brown, 1986.

Blake, C. Fred. "Death and Abuse in Marriage Laments: The Curse of the Chinese Brides." *Asian Folklore Studies* 37 (1978): 13–33.

Blunden, Caroline. *Cultural Atlas of China.* New York: Facts on File, 1983.

Chang, K. C., ed. *Food in Chinese Culture.* New Haven and London: Yale University Press, 1977.

Chen, Weiye, ed. *Flying Dragon and Dancing Phoenix: An Introduction to Selected Chinese Minority Folk Dances.* Beijing: New World Press, 1987.

Cohen, Alvin P. "A Chinese Temple Keeper Talks about Chinese Folk Religion." *Asian Folklore Studies* 36 (1977): 1–17.

———. "Chinese Religion: Popular Religion." *The Encyclopedia of Religion III* (1987): 289–296.

———. "Fiscal Remarks on Some Folk Religion Temples in Taiwan." *Monumenta Serica* 32 (1976): 85–158.

deGroot, Jan Jakob Maria. *The Religious System of China.* 6 vols. Leiden: E. J. Brill, 1892–1910.

Dodwell, Christina. *A Traveller in China.* New York: Beaufort Books, 1985.

Doolittle, Justus. *The Social Life of the Chinese.* New York: Harper and Brothers, 1865.

Dore, Henri. *Researches into Chinese Superstitions.* Translated by M. Kennelly. Shanghai: T'usewei Printing Press, 1914–1920; reprint, Taipei: Ch'eng-wen Publishing Co., 1966.

Eberhard, Wolfram. *A Dictionary of Chinese Symbols.* Translated by G. L. Campbell. London: Routledge & Kegan Paul, 1986.

———. *The Local Cultures of South and East China.* Translated by Alide Eberhard. Leiden: E. J. Brill, 1968.

Ecke, Tseng Yu-ho. *Chinese Folk Art II.* Honolulu: University Press of Hawaii, 1977.

Ha Kuiming, and Ha Yiqi. *Chinese Artistic Kites.* San Francisco: China Books & Periodicals, 1990.

Johnson, David, et al., eds. *Popular Culture in Late Imperial China.* Berkeley: University of California Press, 1985.

Jordan, David K. *Gods, Ghosts, and Ancestors: The Folk Religion of a Taiwanese Village.* Berkeley: University of California Press, 1972.

Lau, Theodore. *The Handbook of Chinese Horoscopes.* New York: Harper and Row, 1980.

Lewis, Paul and Elaine. *Peoples of the Golden Triangle.* New York: Thames and Hudson, 1984.

Liu, Wu-chi, and Irving Yucheng Lo, eds. *Sunflower Splendor.* Garden City, N.Y.: Anchor Press/Doubleday, 1975.

McDougall, Bonnie S., ed. *Popular Chinese Literature and Performing Arts in the People's Republic of China, 1949–1979.* Berkeley: University of California Press, 1984.

Nagel's Encyclopedia-Guide CHINA. Geneva, Switzerland: Nagel Publishers, 1979.

Palmer, Martin, ed. and trans., with Mak Hin Chung, Kwok Man Ho, and Angela Smith. *Tung Shu: The Ancient Chinese Almanac.* Boston: Shambhala, 1986.

Pas, Julian F., ed. *The Turning of the Tide: Religion in China Today.* Oxford and New York: Oxford University Press, 1989.

Sinclair, Kevin. *The Forgotten Tribes of China.* Missisauga, Ontario: Cupress, 1987.

Thompson, Laurence G. "Chinese Religious Year." *The Encyclopedia of Religion III* (1987): 323–328.

———. *The Chinese Way in Religion.* Belmont, Calif.: Dickenson Publishing, 1973.

Wang, Kefen. *The History of Chinese Dance.* Beijing: Foreign Languages Press, 1985.

Weller, Robert P. *Unities and Diversities in Chinese Religion.* Seattle: University of Washington Press, 1987.

Williams, Charles A. *Outlines of Chinese Symbolism.* New York: Julian Press, 1960; first edition, Peiping: Customs College Press, 1931.

Wolf, Arthur P., ed. *Studies in Chinese Society.* Stanford, Calif.: Stanford University Press, 1978.

Wolf, Margery. *Women and the Family in Rural Taiwan.* Stanford, Calif.: Stanford University Press, 1972.

Wong, How Man. *Exploring the Yangtze: China's Longest River.* San Francisco: China Books & Periodicals, 1989.

———. "Peoples of China's Far Provinces." *National Geographic* 165: 3 (1984): 283–333.

Memoirs/History/Asian Studies—
HARD TIME:
THIRTY MONTHS IN A CHINESE LABOR CAMP
Liu Zongren

THE LOS ANGELES TIMES calls Liu's previous works *"warm-hearted and clear-eyed,"* while **THE CHRISTIAN SCIENCE MONITOR SAYS,** *"Mr. Liu has a brand of frankness that during the Cultural Revolution was more likely to win him a stint of hard labor than it was to win him friends."*

Set against the stark backdrop of China's turbulent Cultural Revolution, HARD TIME recounts Liu's experiences during a 30-month internment in Chadian Labor Reform Farm No. 583. Told with a frank and often uncomfortable honesty, the narrative is deeply personal and rooted in the author's loneliness and sudden waves of despair. Along the way, he meets many of China's other "Lost Sons," forming alliances and avoiding enemies.

China Books, 1995
280 pp   0-8351-2542-4 $12.95

Language—
MUTANT MANDARIN:
A GUIDE TO NEW CHINESE SLANG
James J. Wang & Zhou Yimin
Following up the success of his book OUTRAGEOUS CHINESE, James Wang has adapted and enlarged a glossary of new slang published in China by Zhou Yimin, director of the Modern Chinese Research Institute at Beijing Normal University. You'll learn such terms as *Bai-Bai* (from the English "bye-bye," meaning to break up with a lover) and *Mi* (originally "honey from bees" but now like the English "sweetheart"). Includes examples in simplified characters, *pinyin* romanization and English, and a glossary of new Internet and computer terms. Great for language students and those interested in contemporary Chinese society.

China Books, 1995
175 pp   0-8351-2543-2 $12.95

Mutant Mandarin
A Guide to New Chinese Slang

by
Zhou Yimin & James J. Wang

Children/Juvenile—
THE MOON MAIDEN AND OTHER ASIAN FOLKTALES
written & illustrated by Hua Long

Twelve folktales of China and East Asia come alive in this brightly illustrated children's book. These stories are sure to entertain and delight children, while giving important moral lessons. Stories collected include *Li Chi Slays the Serpent*, *The Peacock with the Fiery Tail*, *Sister Lace*, and nine more famous and not-so-famous tales. A great new addition to world folktale collections. *Hua Long is a collective of San Francisco Bay Area artists and writers*.

China Books, 1993   32 pp   full color illustrations
0-8351-2493-2 paper $8.95 0-8351-2494-0 cloth $12.95

Travel/Language —
I CAN READ THAT!
A Traveler's Introduction to Chinese Characters
Julie Mazel Sussman

Tourists in China are often baffled by the many Chinese street signs they see—what do all those characters mean? Now they can have the opportunity to know a good number of those words, thanks to this approach to learning simple words often seen in China. In this richly illustrated book, Julie Mazel Sussman takes you through numbers, names, common words, money, directions, place names, and more. Written in a simple style for non-specialists, I CAN READ THAT! will provide an easy introduction to Chinese for even the most linguistically-impaired.

China Books, 1994
176 pp   0-8351-2533-5   paper $8.95

Classic Literature—
A DREAM OF RED MANSIONS
ABRIDGED ENGLISH EDITION
Cao Xueqin and Gao E, translated by Huang Xinqu

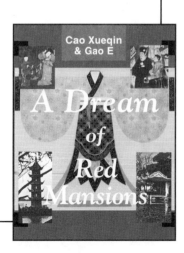

Arguably the greatest work of Chinese fiction, *Hong Lou Meng* has enjoyed a prominent role in world literature for centuries. Many Western readers may be daunted by the 120-chapter, complete version. This new abridged edition however, will make the work more accessible to a wide public. Working from the unabridged Chinese edition, Mr. Huang has focused on the main characters and primary story lines to present a general picture of this masterpiece.

Purple Bamboo Press , 1994
312 pp   0-8351-2529-7   paper $14.95